I fled Him, down the nights and down the days;
   I fled Him, down the arches of the years;
I fled Him, down the labyrinthine ways
   Of my own mind; and in the mist of tears
I hid from Him, and under running laughter.

Francis Thompson,
The Hound of Heaven

Act of
Contrition

PERSONAL RESPONSIBILITY AND SIN

Jeffrey Sobosan, C.S.C.

Ave Maria Press
Notre Dame, Indiana 46556

This book is for Paul

Permission

Absolution by Jeffrey G. Sobosan, copyright 1976 by Christian
Century Foundation. Reprinted by permission from the February
18, 1976, issue of *The Christian Century*.

Nihil Obstat

Most Reverend Paul E. Waldschmidt, C.S.C.
Censor Deputatus

Imprimatur

Most Reverend Cornelius M. Power, D.D., J.C.D.
Archbishop of Portland in Oregon

© 1979 by Ave Maria Press, Notre Dame, Indiana 46556

International Standard Book Number: 0-87793-188-7 (cloth)
0-87793-189-5 (paperback)

Library of Congress Catalog Card Number: 79-54695

Manufactured in the United States of America.

Contents

Preface

All of us are aware that we commit sin. We need no reminding of the wrongdoing that plagues our lives, the vice that too often marks our thoughts, feelings and deeds. Like a stinging wound it is there, this sin and wrongdoing and vice; like a laughing demon it will remain. It is a part of us, and we must willingly come to grips with it.

In this book I will be arguing—or more correctly, suggesting—that contrition is the way we come to grips with sin, the wrongdoing and vice that mark our existence. Contrition is the attitude or state of mind in which the individual is not only aware of his or her sin, but is impelled to do something about it. It is an active attitude, rather than a passive one, a state of mind that is meant to issue in movement, to produce results. Hence the appropriateness, I think, of the word "act" in the title of this book, *Act of Contrition*.

There are several bases upon which a reflection on contrition could rest. It could, for example, be based strictly on biblical analysis, or on case studies, or on the history of doctrine and spirituality. What I have chosen as my basis, however, is none of these singly but all of them together, as they find expression in the sources, the personal experiences, from which I have drawn inspiration.

But still we may ask: Why make an act of contrition at all; what impels an individual to confess that he has sinned? In the following three chapters I hope to provide an answer to this question. I will do so by reflecting on three further questions, each occupying a successive chapter of its own. The first question (chapter one): To whom do we make our act of contrition? To it we respond: to God and other human beings. The second question (chapter two): What do we confess in contrition? To it we respond: our excessive self-concern. The third question (chapter three): For what do we ask in contrition? To it we respond: the prayer of others. In the course of asking and answering each of these questions in turn I hope to provide a composite answer to the single question: Why confess contrition at all?

But if someone were still to insist that I capsulize here and now the motive underlying our act of contrition, I would respond somewhat reluctantly (because too briefly): the experience of guilt. By this I would mean the experience of having committed some moral wrong, according to whatever moral code the individual affirms. For professing Christians, let us say—since they are the ones with whom this book is preeminently concerned—this moral code would clearly involve the pattern of behavior enshrined in the words and deeds of Jesus. Additionally, individuals would have to understand the moral wrong as something for which they themselves are culpable, that is, something for which they personally deserve blame or censure. We could never speak, for example, of an infant experiencing guilt, even though he may manifest in his behavior a selfishness that clearly offends our moral code. Nor, more generally, would someone experience guilt if the moral breach he or she commits is understood as praiseworthy, not blameworthy. Guilt that issues in personal contrition is experienced only on the basis of an awareness, however dim or lucid, that the individual has by his or her own responsibility veered from a pattern of behavior believed (because it has been taught to be and/or personally determined to be) good and worthy of obedience.

How does an individual come to experience such guilt? It cannot be our purpose here to explore the psychological or sociological subtleties involved in a complete answer. But any answer, I think, must at least acknowledge what we said above about culpability. We can experience guilt only as we become convinced that we have committed a moral wrong against some given moral code. Sometimes this conviction is born from within. Its source is personal conscience—that familiar "inner voice," the trained or intuitive awareness that speaks clear judgment on our behavior. In this case no external persuasion is required to convince us that we have broken our moral code. Our offense is as clear to us as the noonday sun.

At other times, though, external persuasion is required. Because our awareness of the moral code is insufficient, let us say, or self-serving, some source outside our consciences must guide us to the conviction that our behavior constitutes a moral offense. Of course, the success of this whole process presumes from the start that we have become—or can be induced to become—receptive enough to accept this external guidance in the shaping of our consciences. Otherwise all the persuasive talent in the world— all the wit and wisdom the guide can exercise—will fall on deaf ears. Conviction cannot be given to people, or forced upon them. They must arrive at it for themselves.

Spirituality attempts to provide the individual with guidance that will lead to personal conviction. Sometimes this will take fairly exact forms. The conviction the spirituality attempts to elicit, for example, will involve particular political issues, or medical or sexual or ecological issues. In these cases some singular lack of integrity, knowledge or discretion is noted in the behavior of individuals, and the purpose of the spirituality is to bring this lack to awareness and encourage specific alterations in patterns of behavior.

The purpose of the following chapters, however, is much more general than this—and perhaps more difficult. They are not designed to focus on any single issue that offends my judgment of what constitutes right behavior. Instead, while often using specific examples, my purpose is to provide a blanket reflection on the fact that we do indeed act wrongly—that we do sin—frequently and in many different ways; that our contrition is a confession of this fact; and that this confession always implies an awareness of personal responsibility in the contrite individual. Whether this purpose is fulfilled, whether these chapters in fact elicit conviction, is for the reader to decide. I can only engage the task of spirituality—to provide persuasive guidance—as best I can.

One final introductory note. While writing this book I have frequently reminded myself of the fact that grasshoppers can only see things that are in motion. Why? Because, like the grasshopper, every individual has a limited consciousness in that his only means of relating to himself and the world around him is through a given frame of reference—or what we might also call a certain rubric of understanding. It will quickly become obvious that the major frame of reference within which I examine the phenomenon of contrition is my own understanding of the Christian spiritual life, the person and message of Christ, be it true or misguided in the opinion of others. I say this, however, not so much in apology as in recognition of the fact that my own vision, like that of every grasshopper and every man, is also limited.

December 8, 1978
A Feast of Mary
The University of Portland

I.
To Whom Do We Make Our Act of Contrition?

In much of today's Christian spirituality, and throughout its finest traditions, we are trained to consider the plural, the "we," over the singular, the "I." We are taught that Christian life must be other-oriented rather than self-oriented; that concern for our "brothers and sisters" takes precedence over self-concern. With this tradition we have no argument; indeed, we will sustain it as one of the guiding themes in the following reflections.

1. The Importance of the "I"

For the present moment it is the "I" alone that matters. It is the "I" that sets the stage for our act of contrition. It indicates that I am taking responsibility for what follows: that *I* am confessing it. It is not "we"; I do not share with others what I am going to confess. I speak it *to* them, as we will see, but I speak only *for* myself.

11

The "I" means that I cannot seek refuge in a crowd when declaring my contrition. Instead, I must stand alone. My contrition is not shared. I am not contrite for others; I do not include them as partners in my sin. The responsibility for it is my own; the blame is my own. How others may have contributed to this sin is for them to confess. I cannot speak for them; I can speak only for myself.

Yet we will also see that the "I" places me in a relationship with others. I can speak this word "I" only because there are others who are distinct from me, with whom I live and relate. It is *how* I have done so, in fact, that generally informs my confession of sin. Have I lived or related well or ill with them?

But again—for the moment—it is the "I" alone that matters to us. The speaking of the word "I" forms the burden of contrition. For are we not all inclined to take full responsibility only for the praiseworthy in our lives, and to share our sins with others? But by this word "I" we refuse this inclination, this seeking consolation in the sins of others and how they have influenced us. We acknowledge that we alone have brought ourselves to where we are: to the point where we must be contrite for what we have been or done. Our only consolation in this is our awareness that our sins are not hidden and festering, spreading unaware throughout our spirit. They are conscious in our confession. But then, of course—if we know that our sins have been our own doing—we know that their amendment is also within our grasp.

This last point will occupy us at great length later on. For now we may simply note that with sin a situation prevails similar to that found in the common, always sad example of alcoholism. The first step in any alcoholic's recovery is the realization that his disease, as well as its cure, is basically his own responsibility; that neither can be fairly passed off onto another. Before the bottle on the table the alcoholic stands alone, just as the sinner does before his or her sin. And redemption in either case is made possible the more the individual becomes involved in the redeeming process.

Now throughout the following pages we will also have to temper somewhat our understanding of the individual's responsibility for his sin. We will see, for example, that this responsibility does not always imply culpability. By this I mean that, while it is indeed the individual who commits sin, we cannot conclude that his sin is always committed deliberately or conscientiously or—to borrow a judicial phrase—"with malice aforethought." Sometimes sin is the result of ignorance, sometimes of a momentary but blind fury, sometimes of psychological moods of maladjustment— for none of which the individual can be fairly blamed.

We need to remain aware, after all, that each of us is the heir of "original sin"—that there are "blind spots" in our minds and wills that make us "do what we would not do" (Rom 7:15). But whether we are culpable or not, the point I wish to make is that the sin we commit is still our responsibility; we have committed it and no one else. Nor are we condemned to this sin, as if chained inescapably to an endlessly turning wheel. For we have the power, I believe, to open our eyes and see clearly even the "blind spots" in our existence—so that we may master not only the intentional but unintentional, the willing and unwitting sins we commit. This power, I will later suggest, derives from the revelation that occurred in the deeds and destiny of Jesus Christ.

The speaking of the "I" in contrition, therefore, has this positive cast: The sin within us is not uncontrollable. Otherwise we would be speaking in the plural. The sin would be in our surrounding world, which we cannot control, and we would be its unwitting or unwilling participants. But the "I" intends to disassociate us from this surrounding world—at least regarding the question of responsibility. It asserts that accountability for the sin we commit is ours, without recourse to factors external to us, before which we are powerless.

But here, of course, we must digress a moment; for there is obviously a sense in which we may indeed depersonalize the question of responsibility for sin. We may say of a child, for example, that he is "born into sin." The phrase functions as a qualifier of human existence. The New Testament draws a distinction between "sin" (sometimes with a capital S) and "sins." The former is the condition that the latter express in particular acts. It is the *milieu,* so to speak, the "atmosphere" which is conducive to the specific, concrete wrongs that human beings commit. But the distinction so stated—as the difference between "sin" and "sins"—is one I have always found verbally difficult. So, in an effort at clarity, I will speak throughout these reflections of "fault" as the milieu in which "sins" occur. What I mean specifically by this distinction, though, cannot presently occupy us. That will have to await our extended discussion of it in chapter two.

To return to our main point: The question of contrition cannot arise whenever we understand ourselves as the prey of uncontrollable forces operating in our lives. We would then be perpetually excused by the authority and power of these forces. In truth, we can be contrite only when we have a choice regarding what we do, a free choice, without compulsion. Otherwise the experience of contrition would make no sense—save perhaps to indicate mental illness. For whenever we view what we are or what we do as determined by forces beyond our control, we are best described as "instruments" rather than responsible agents. We are not responsible for our hunger, for example, or our need for sleep; these are "forces" outside our influence. But we are responsible for our pride and lack of generosity. We are not responsible for our having been born and our having to die, but we are responsible for the seriousness with which we take our faith in God. We cannot be contrite for our hunger and weariness, our birth and death; but we can be contrite for our lack of love and humility.

The speaking of the "I," then, which places us in a relationship of contrition toward others, involves those elements within this relationship that we can control. The fact that I have been born black or white or yellow, in Africa, America or Vietnam, does not include these elements. The fact, however, that I have been kind or cruel to others around me does.

There is no such thing as an uncontrollably good or uncontrollably evil individual. We cannot universalize the fact that we are determined in some respects to include what we are in all respects. That is the great myth, the shibboleth of naive bio-behaviorism. In ages we have left behind, the wickedness and sins an individual committed were often excused by invoking the power of savage demons, nymphs and spirits he could not control. The influence attributed to malefic gods in ancient literature is well known. Now our names are more sophisticated. The demons we invoke are injustice, inheritance, neurosis, and so on. But the conclusion remains the same: Our sin is not our own doing, or at least not completely our own doing.

The "I" that is spoken in contrition denies this conclusion. For in speaking it I affirm my complete responsibility over the activities for which I am contrite. In contrition I am *in extremis*. I know that all my excuses are gone, and that I must now face the fact: I have done this, and no one else. Reluctantly, sometimes very reluctantly, I must succumb to the conclusion: Let me no longer try to blame others for my sin, or the circumstances of my birth, or my social position, or my education. Let me stand alone and face the fact that I am accountable for what I have done. Do I not willingly accept praise for the virtue I possess, not wishing to share it with others? Let me now accept responsibility for my vice without sharing it.

It is precisely here, as we said, at the point of this last statement, that we discover the redeeming character, the positive cast, of our act of contrition. For in confessing that I have done wrong of my own accord, I am asserting at the same time that I have the power to do right. We are dealing with one coin that has two sides.

Acknowledging Responsibility

An example might be helpful here—not to demonstrate contrition for sin, but the simple awareness of responsibility that must underlie any individual's free activity. Let us imagine a boy, say, of eight or nine years. We all know how at this age a youngster can spend hours with a set of building blocks. In his imagination he conceives an edifice and sets out on the task of contructing it. But at some point, let us say, the edifice begins to wobble, and the child, refusing to accept the reason why—refusing to accept, for instance, his failure to plan adequately, his inexperience and lack of talent—reacts frantically. But try as he might, the wobble increases until the whole uncompleted structure comes crashing down. The boy's response is one of fury. He blames everything for the failure but his own ineptitude: The blocks were made unevenly; his luck went awry; some "devil" is playing perverse tricks on him; and so on. He goes to any length seeking causes for the mess now at his feet, all the while refusing to acknowledge that it was self-induced. He stubbornly denies that the responsibility for the failed building is his own, that he cannot pass his failure onto or share it with anything outside himself. Instead, he seeks consolation in the thought that nothing is wrong with him—his plans and talent are adequate—but with factors beyond his control. In this all-but-automatic attitude of self-concern—here expressed as placing blame on anyone or anything but oneself—we begin to get a glimpse of the meaning of fault as we will describe it in chapter two. Fault, we will say, resides in excessive self-concern.

And so the boy begins again building in the same way as before. Because he does not admit that the responsibility for the initial failure was his own, he follows unchanged his same plans and procedure. He is certain that this time he will succeed, if nothing again interferes. Only with another mishap, and possibly many more besides, might he begin to recognize that the responsibility for his failure cannot be sloughed off on external causes. This, of course, is part of that whole painful complex of the growth process we call maturing. In time, if he develops normally, the child will acknowledge that he alone is accountable for his failures, without the consoling benefit of refusing or sharing the accountability. At this point in his life he will begin to learn something of what it means to say "I" when making his act of contrition.

Until now we have been using various expressions to describe contrition, the act of declaring guilt or responsibility for wrongdoing. I would now like to further the discussion by introducing the idea of "confessing contrition." In this context, what does it mean to "confess"? The word derives from the Latin verb *confiteri,* which in turn is two words combined, *con* plus *fiteri. Con* is here employed as an intensive prefix; it is used to emphasize the meaning of the word to which it is attached. So our concern is with the word *fiteri.* In its primary usage the word means "to admit" or "to acknowledge"; in its secondary usage it means "to reveal." To confess something, then, is to admit or acknowledge or reveal it outrightly, without excuse or abridgement. It is to say, "I own up to this," and to say no more. It is to take complete responsibility for a deed or a thought or a feeling. The intensive prefix, as we said, serves only to stress this taking of responsibility. It attempts to capture, for example, the experience one might have not just of admitting but of shouting out one's responsibility for all to hear, or of writing it down. It is like the public confession of sins that the Israelites repeatedly make before God, as we read, for example, in Nehemiah 9:1-2:

> Now on the twenty-fourth day of the month the people of Israel were assembled with fasting and in sackcloth, and stood and confessed their sins, and with earth upon their heads. They separated themselves from all foreigners, and stood and confessed their sins with loud shouts.

We may say, therefore, that to confess responsibility for one's deeds, thoughts, or feelings is not to hold it secret, in one's heart. It is to publicize it, in the sense of acknowledging it before at least one other. *Confession is always an act revealing to another something for which we take responsibility.* This will be our operative definition throughout these reflections. Confession is not, in other words, something like our daydreams, about which we can speak privately to ourselves. Instead, it turns outward, away from us; its force, its movement, is always centrifugal. When someone like Shakespeare's Hamlet, for example, speaks to himself of his plans and pains, he is not by our definition engaging in confession. In dramatic jargon he is performing a soliloquy, whereas confession would require a colloquy.

Now it is clear that within the above description of confession the issue of sin has yet to be directly raised. At this point the individual may be confessing *either* virtue or vice, the good or evil done. He or she may be confessing to philanthropy or to crime, a desire to help or a desire to hurt. Within this basic description, confession has the minimal function of being only a public avowal that the individual is taking responsibility for himself, his thoughts, feelings and deeds. And we may note again—this "public" need not be constituted by great crowds of listening people; it may frequently be constituted by just one person, a single listener. What makes the avowal public is simply that it is no longer held in secret, but brought out of oneself and shared.

Judgment on this avowal, of course, may vary. When an individual confesses his or her vice, for example, we are generally inclined to consider it a praiseworthy act. But when he or she confesses virtue we tend to view it as an act of conceit. The first confession we usually judge a product of humility and selflessness; the second a product of self-concern and pride. Each is a confession, though, because each is a public admission of responsibility.

It is only when the act of confession also becomes an act of contrition that its limits are narrowed to those of sin and wrongdoing. Or more briefly: Contrition is the confession of sin. It is the acknowledgment that one has failed morally, the public revelation that one has thought, felt, or acted wrongly—however this might be defined. But it is also more than this. Contrition is also the avowal that as I have committed this wrong, so I can *and will* rectify it. Contrition always involves this possibility of amendment. Without it the individual could only mourn his sins and succumb to their inevitability. He could do nothing about them; he would be trapped in a revolving wheel of failures.

Willingness to Change

A brief examination of dictionary definitions indicates the way amendment is integrated into the notion of contrition. If we go to *Webster's* we find contrition defined as the state of being "broken down with sorrow for sin, humbly and thoroughly repentant"; or more simply, "sincere repentance." The word comes from the Latin *terere,* meaning "grind" or "bruise," plus the intensive prefix *con.* If we then look up "repent" as the basis of the key word "repentance" in defining contrition, we find: 1. "to amend or resolve to amend one's life as a result of contrition for one's sins"; 2. "to change one's mind with regard to past or intended action, conduct, etc., on account of regret or dissatisfaction"; 3. "to feel regret, contrition, or compunction, for what one has done or omitted to do." Repentance is consequently defined as: "act of repenting, or state of being penitent; specifically contrition for sins, *with amendment for life"* (my italics).

To confess with contrition, then, if amendment is indeed a part of contrition, is to acknowledge not only that one has acted wrongly, but that this wrongful behavior can be righted. This, we may otherwise say, constitutes the *hope* involved in confessing contrition. It is to assert: "I who have sinned in this way am not condemned by necessity to continue in my sin; I have the power within me to overcome it, to replace my vice with virtue." It is to recognize that one can change.

Of course, this is not an easy recognition; or more exactly, it is not a recognition that is easily effected or put into practice. Honest reflection reveals in each of us, after all, a certain moral or spiritual inertia. It expresses itself in the variously similar statements: I cannot change; I am too old to change; this is the way I was raised; I am this way by nature. Contrition demands the breaking of this inertia. It demands not only the recognition that one can change, but the willingness and consistent attempt to do so. Otherwise, of course, it remains sterile, void of purpose.

Let us return to our example. Once the boy reaches the point of being able to say "I" in confessing his failure, he may begin his task anew. But now he will know that his edifice has continually toppled not because there was some teasing demon or bad luck or misshapen blocks causing it. Rather, the failure has been in him: in the way he has persisted in placing the blocks; in his refusal to see that they could rise only so high before collapsing under his inadequate construction. Instead of repeating the same mistakes, because he excused himself from his failure, he now learns from his mistakes. He sees that they have been his own— but that if this is so, then the power to correct them is also his own. He need no longer placate some vexing demon, or blame imagined defects in his material, or wish for better luck—all these while continuing to build as before. He need only take responsibility for his failure, admit it as his own, and change his pattern of construction.

So he now restructures the foundation and various stages of the building, and finds that with each restructuring he comes closer to completing his task. And at last he does. The boy succeeds, and in the process has begun to understand the meaning of contrition. He now knows something of what it means to recognize and admit that he himself, and no one else, has failed in the goal he set for himself; he has learned something of the meaning of regret. Likewise he has learned something of the meaning of amendment: that he *can* change his "ways," his patterned method of acting. Even more, he has learned that he *must* change his ways—that it is not an option—so long as he continues in the desire to succeed at his task and accomplish his goal. Otherwise his learning remains unapplied; it has gone for naught—he still finds himself in a spinning circle of the same failures.

As he grows older and matures, the child gradually discovers that this experience of contrition is not limited solely to his childish games. He realizes that it has a much broader compass in his life. With each growing year he finds that the "I" he speaks in confessing contrition has a greater extension than the year before; that he must apply it in ever-widening areas of his life. Once he realizes this, however, he also becomes aware that he cannot go back, cannot retreat to the consolation he once had: that it was not "I" who did this, but someone or something else. He cannot succumb to nostalgia for his childhood years, as the time when he remained innocent of all wrongdoing because he was ignorant of his responsibility for it. With the assertion of the "I" in confessing contrition, the individual loses both his innocence and his ignorance. He leaves behind the daydream world of childhood wherein he thought he could do no wrong—that wrong was always done to him—and enters that harsher world of self-knowledge wherein he must account for the wrong he has done. Instead of blaming others for his failure, he now confesses it to them. And should the failure have involved these others, should he have sinned or done wrong in their regard, he not only confesses it to them, but confesses it with contrition.

Therefore, regarding the question *to whom* the individual confesses contrition—if, as we said, confession is to admit, acknowledge, or reveal something *to* someone—we have our initial answer: to the person one has sinned against and wronged. It is to this person that we all must go whenever we confess with contrition. It is to him or her that we must express ourselves with repentance for the wrong we have committed, and with resolve to amend this wrong.

Our purpose in the following two sections will be to reflect further on this initial answer, so as to amplify its meaning. Following the pattern outlined in the preface, we will do so when the other to whom we address our confession is thought to be, first God, and secondly, other human beings.

2. **Contrition Before God**

To some extent all of us engage in personal dialogue with ourselves. It is as if we were two people, the one speaking to the other, giving advice, passing judgment, and so on. This is no unhealthy split within our personalities, no schizophrenia to cause us worry. It is a normal, quite typical technique that we all now and then employ in reaching decisions and forming opinions. One part of us must sometimes play the challenger of another part, the devil's advocate. For one pattern of thought within us there must be a protagonist for another pattern—if we hope to make intelligent and committed decisions. For a defender of our actions there must be a prosecutor—if we hope to advance in moral rectitude.

We must not become trapped, in other words, in just one way of thinking. This becomes particularly urgent whenever we tend to consider it the only, or only worthwhile, way of thinking. Before our mind's eye we must learn always to place options, possible alternatives to viewpoints, opinions, beliefs we hold. We must learn, then, to expand our horizons sideways, to see in more than just one direction. Because it is precisely this ability, I would now say, that allows us to see that we are in sin. We understand that we have acted wrongly whenever we can say to ourselves: This other action would have been to act rightly. Without this consciousness of alternatives, trapped in only one way of thinking, the question of right and wrong, virtue and vice, cannot arise.

In the above sense, of course, whenever we admit a sin it might be that we are only speaking to ourselves. "Now you have done this," we might say, "and it was wrong. You must amend your ways." But as soon as our admission becomes a *confession of contrition,* the situation changes. For this confession, as we said, implies sorrow because the sin has had as its object another outside ourselves. It is *I* who have sinned in *your* regard; *I* have failed *you* in what I have thought, felt or done. When confessing contrition, therefore, it is never enough to speak only to oneself. The individual must also speak to the other whom he or she has offended.

So far, then, we may say that confessing contrition involves the individual in a double movement. First, it involves a placing of options before the mind's eye, because of which one can choose to act wrongly rather than rightly—whatever the given vision of right and wrong might be. Secondly, it involves the individual in a relationship of sorrow or regret toward the one wronged, with the concomitant desire to amend the wrong. Both these movements will occupy us at great length in the pages to come.

An unbroken tradition of Christian spirituality asserts that in the first instance the other to whom we confess contrition is God. Whenever one sins the sin initially sets the person in a relationship with God, and it is to God that we must first confess our regret and desire to amend. The tradition affirms that this is so because it is to God that we owe our first responsibility for what we are and do, because it is to God that we owe the origin and sustenance of our very lives. Christian faith indeed affirms not only that God has given life to us, but that for this life we must account, not just now and then but always.

Of course, we may still do with our lives whatever we wish: That is not the point here. Every gift, if it is given freely, may be used however the recipient chooses. The recipient is not forced or constrained to use it only in certain ways. We may cherish or abuse it, for example, hoard or share it: The choice is freely and obviously ours. But however we use the gift, we must also be aware of and accept the fair possibility that we will need to answer for our use to the giver.

This faith in God as giver cannot be proved; it can only be affirmed. There is no compelling demonstration requiring the idea that we must acknowledge, admit or reveal our activities before God. But this faith not only makes such confession possible; it demands it without option. Faith asserts that God does not give us life only to withdraw from the gift. On the contrary, God remains actively involved with our life, permanently concerned with how it is used. Our confession of contrition to him is one response to this concern.

Images of God

Now such confession may obviously occur in a variety of ways, depending on how God is understood. An individual, for example, who envisions God as a somewhat picayune old man will confess his contrition with meticulous precision. He does not leave out a single item of wrong in what he has thought, felt and done. His God wants to know all, and all in detail. This precision is engaged, however, not so much because the individual is afraid of God. It is more that he doesn't want to "hurt" God by leaving something out of God's confidence. He feels an obligation to satisfy God's inquisitiveness.

This whole image, of course, is a rather depressing, childish one—though it is amazing how many cling to it in practice. It is based on an attitude similar to that a son might take toward his lonely old father. He tells his father all the details of events that have happened during the course of a day or week or a month in order to make the old man feel a part of what has happened. Sharing in this way, the son thinks, will give his father a sense of belonging, of participating in his child's life. It is the son's way of accounting to his father for the years of free love and devotion, the gift, that his father has given him.

To some extent, I suspect, the above image gains ground the more an individual shies away from the following one. Here God is again envisioned as a picayune old man. Only this time he is not merely curious; he is also mean, even savage. The individual not only does not, he dares not forget his sins in confessing before God, lest God become not hurt but furious. Every detail must be gone over scrupulously; failure to mention all is to commit sacrilege and invite punishment. Needless to say, this image is even more distressing than the first. It invokes unreasoned fear and trembling in the individual. He confesses because he is afraid for himself; he is contrite because he is terrified of what God might otherwise do to him. He thinks that his confession and contrition will somehow assuage God's ever-ready anger.

There is, we all know, ample testimony for the above image of God throughout religious literature—including that of Christianity. In the bible itself, for example, in the Old Testament story of Asa (cf. 2 Sm 6:1-11), we have a frightening instance of this God's swift and terrible anger toward even a justifiable exception to his law. Briefly, the story relates how it was considered sacrilege to touch, under any but the most restricted circumstances, the holy Ark of the Covenant. But in procession one day the Ark begins to wobble and fall. Asa, shocked at the possibility of the even greater sacrilege of an Ark bruised and dirtied on the ground, moves quickly to brace it. But does his God smile; does his God excuse? No, instead, God too moves quickly, striking Asa dead on the spot. Tolerating no exception to his law, no matter how minor or justifiable, is it any wonder that confession to such a God would include every possible detail of wrongdoing? His fury would be worth the pain of a life of studied scrupulosity.

It is fundamentally the same case—on a much more commonplace level—with any child who has a too strict father. When the child misbehaves he hurries to tell his father, and tell in great detail, what he has done—if he does not try to hide it first. Why?—not because he has hurt or disappointed his father, certainly not because of his love for some abstract Good he has offended. The reason is a far simpler one: The child is afraid. He is afraid of the punishment that will follow his misbehavior. And he thinks that if of his own accord he "owns up" to what he has done, the punishment will either be rescinded or at least considerably lightened. He confesses with contrition, in short, for his own sake.

On the surface the child's actions are easily understandable. Fear of punishment is doubtlessly a powerful motive for contrition, especially when it is combined with the possibility of mercy in the one offended. In fact, we have built up a whole psychological bias in this regard. Are we not usually, almost spontaneously, inclined to believe that no matter how serious our wrong, honesty and contrition about it has an ameliorating effect on the one wronged? In this way, so we think, the sting is pulled (to whatever extent) on the punishment.

What is lacking in the above attitude is what I would call, following the words of Jesus (Mt 5:8), "purity of heart." By this I mean that with such an attitude we are double-minded. We confess with contrition the deed we have done, not because the deed itself is wrong, but because we are frightened of the punishment it will bring. It is the same as when we do what is good, not for the sake of the good itself but for the sake of a reward. If we were pure in heart, on the other hand, we would be contrite precisely because our deeds were wrong, without consideration for the question of whether or not punishment will follow. Before God we would confess our deeds, not because of what God might do if we do not, but purely because *we have committed the deed, and the deed was wrong.* We would see this confession, as we said, as part of our responsibility before God for God's having given and sustained our life. Or differently put: Our confession would be born from neither pity nor fear of God, as in the first two cases above, but from our awareness that our use of the gift of our life merits accountability before its Giver.

The upshot of this emphasis on purity of heart is that the individual need not confess all the minutiae of his wrongdoing. For this would only indicate that he has slipped back to, or never really left, his condition of scrupulosity before a too curious or too fearful God. Rather, his task is to confess the particular *sin* he has committed—such as pride or venality, blind anger or indifference—not all its grim, distasteful details. It is the specific sin, not the specific scenario, that the individual must responsibly confess with contrition to God.

God's Power, Our Power

What motivates an individual to confess contrition to God at all? Not fear, as we have said, and certainly not pity. Rather, I would like to suggest—in light of remarks made in the previous section—that the individual, if pure in heart, is contrite for this reason, and this alone: gratitude. We are contrite out of thankfulness to God. And we are thankful, as we said, first because God has given and sustains our very lives, and secondly because God has given us the freedom of an "I," an identity that allows us to do as we will. If we have committed sin, therefore, our contrition before God will be a grateful one—not for the sin, to be sure, but for that very freedom which, having led us into sin, can lead us away from it.

Without this freedom, no amendment of life is possible. It is what prevents the individual from becoming trapped in sin, unable to rectify the wrong done. Or differently: If we say that what constitutes our identity is the prevailing freedom with which we can structure our existence—the particular values we choose, the way we express what we think, feel or do—then by that same freedom we can re-structure these values. We may do so, of course, to the benefit of vice, increasing the wrong that we think, feel or do. This is always an option. But by the same token, we may also do so to the benefit of virtue, repenting the wrong we commit and amending it. This, too, is just as much an option for us. And it is for this option, the second one, that we have gratitude when we confess contrition to God.

It is for the above reasons that I would now suggest that the attribute most adequately describing God when confessing contrition to him is "almighty," or "omnipotent." At first we might think the attribute would more appropriately be "all-knowing," or "omniscient," since to confess is to acknowledge, admit, reveal; in short, to make known. The matching attribute in God to the human act of confession would seem logically to be the quality of God's own knowledge—for then we would be affirming God's direct involvement in the act of confession itself. Our acknowledgment of what we have thought, felt or done would consequently need to be proportionate to God's own knowledge of these things. Our confession could never be an acknowledgment of something of which God was somehow unaware.

One of the obvious, and I think beneficial, results accruing from this emphasis on God's omniscience would be the diminishment of the ever-present temptation not to confess all, to hold things back. When God is understood as all-knowing, it is plainly ill-considered to think that he could be deceived, or given only part of the truth. On the other hand, there is a danger in this emphasis insofar as it can reduce confession to a game of integrity: to see how honest the individual is; if he can bring himself to tell all. Or worse, it can reduce confession to a game of memory: to see how bright the individual is; if he can remember all. In either case the individual's relationship with God has clearly gone awry, as any game relationship with God must. It has established a competition between God and the individual's integrity or memory, in which God's omniscience is the antagonist to be matched and stalemated.

In the above situation, moreover, we are easily led back to the image of God previously discussed. Only now God is not just a curious, mean old man; he is also an omniscient one. He knows *all* our sins and wrongdoings, and contrition becomes a test to see if we regret and desire to amend them all. In this image God is envisioned as lurking, waiting for us to forget just one thing. Then he screams, "Sacrilege! You have not told all; you have held back. Why haven't you remembered everything, all your sins? Is it not important to you that you have committed sin? Are your sins so insignificant that you have fallen prey to the luxury of forgetfulness?"

Though imaginative, and only that, the above recitation is still a bit frightening. The language may be too irritated, too petulant in tone to capture a convincing representation of God speaking. But the idea underlying the language is what frightens us: the idea that we will be held accountable not only for all our sins, but for all their particularities. It is the little word, the word "all," that strikes our fear. It incorporates the whole world of our existence, our complete identities, everything we are: our thoughts, feelings and deeds.

But who can remember all? Who wishes to remember all, every sin and the details of each? One remembers what he can, the sins that stand out, that are important to him. It is for these that he is contrite. He confesses with contrition what matters to him in his relationship with God; his infidelity toward how he believes he should act before God. But not, certainly not, every single infidelity, and every single time it has marked his thoughts, feelings or deeds. God may know these things, but is it important that each be reiterated to him in detail? Is God an omniscient accountant, checking off what has been confessed and what has not? The image is repellent.

The above paragraphs offer a brief psychological description of an attitude that one understanding of God as omniscient might easily create in an individual. It is a disturbing attitude, I would think, for anyone who considers ego-obsession (that is, too great a concern with one's own self) to be contrary to the Christian spirit. Of course, how responsible the individual might be for this state of mind, and its correlative image of God, is another and quite difficult question. As noted before, there is no doubt that a fervid and long-standing school of Christian spirituality, buttressed by ecclesiastical authority, has profoundly encouraged it.

Let us take the specific case, for instance, of a Catholic priest in the "confessional." What is it that he hears for the most part, if not a litany of particulars? How many sins have I committed; how serious were they; how many times did I commit them? These must be the type of detailed questions the confessing individual asks himself, since his confession is an answer to each of them. Then, at the end, the most convincing word of all: I confess these sins, *and all those I cannot remember*. He feels obliged to confess even what he does not know. But how can this be? How can an individual admit, acknowledge, reveal what he does not know? And why would God, or anyone, possibly hold him to account for it?

It is exactly the above approach to contrition that we are trying to overcome by suggesting that confession should be addressed not to "omniscient" God, but to "almighty" God. I say this because in one sense the relationship established between the individual and God in contrition is precisely one of power. At first this may sound somewhat odd; at worst it may even send shivers through our minds. "Power," after all, is not a very pleasant word. Its meaning is too frequently ambivalent; the contexts in which it is used are too often distressing. In what follows, then, the burden is clearly mine. And while asking indulgence in advance for leaving many questions unanswered, I will try to explain briefly what I mean by relating contrition to power.

The approach returns us once again to the issue of the "I" when confessing contrition to God. As we argued in the last section, whenever we speak the "I" of confession we are claiming responsibility for what we are admitting, acknowledging, revealing. But, as we also noted a few pages ago, to claim this responsibility is at the same time to assert our freedom. For responsibility cannot exist without freedom.

But what at root is freedom if not power: the power to effect one's will, to keep or discard, to affirm or deny? In confessing our contrition to God, we are recognizing that we are free: that we have the power to place ourselves in sin; that we have the power to rectify this situation; that we have the power to effect our choices. Contrition breaks down the excesses of determinism, in other words, or else it makes no sense. The individual could not intelligently regret and seek to amend his wrongdoing if he thought himself powerless before the influence of behavioral patterns.

It is the almightiness of God, God's freedom and power, from which our own freedom and power emerge. When we confess contrition to God it is this idea, I think, that we are recognizing. We are acknowledging that the freedom which is ours, even the freedom to act wrongly, finds its source in God. Or otherwise put, it is because God shares with us what is his own, that we ourselves are free. Our power to act rightly or wrongly, our freedom, is thus derived; it is a gift, something drawn from outside ourselves. But like all gifts, as we said before, it may be either cherished or abused.

When we confess contrition to God, therefore, we are essentially confessing the uses to which we have put our freedom. And we are contrite because these uses have entailed abuses of the power of our freedom. Before God we have acted wrongly; freely we have given power to the vice within us rather than the virtue. It is this that we admit in confessing our contrition; it is this that we regret and freely resolve to avoid in the future. To be contrite is to affirm our power over our existence. It is to deny that we are mere playthings in what we think, feel and do.

3. Contrition Before Our Brothers and Sisters

In faith we relate primarily to God. The first object of faith, its beating heart, is a personal relationship with God. This faith asks that in some fashion God be conceptualized in terms with human referents. He must be understood, for example, as a God who "hears" us, who "responds" to us, who is "involved" with our lives; in short, a God with whom we can relate as we relate to other persons. It is, I think, precisely this need for a personal relationship when confessing contrition that involves us not only in the personhood of God, but in the personhood of other human beings. It is just as possible to be in sin before other human beings, our brothers and sisters, as it is to be in sin before God. And for this sin it becomes just as necessary to confess contrition before them as it is to confess contrition before God. Within any personal relationship where we have thought, felt or done wrongly—whether it be within our relationship to God or our relationship to another human being—we must confess sorrow for the wrong and the intention to amend it. The phrase we have been using, "brothers and sisters," is meant to acknowledge this idea. As we will see more thoroughly later on, its referent is obviously not a biological one. The phrase is far more inclusive, meaning all those persons other than God whom we have wronged and before whom we must confess our contrition.

In fact, sin is doubtlessly specified more often with regard to our brothers and sisters than it is with regard to God. The particular context of our sin is more frequently our relationship with other human beings—how we live with and respond to them—than our relationship with God. We cannot, after all, be merciless toward God or fail to care for his needs; we cannot ruin his hopes or cause him despair. These ideas, at least within a Christian theology, make no sense. Our contrition, then, while it may initially be directed toward God for the failure to pursue virtue rather than vice in our lives, must broaden out from this point to include the many specific wrongs we commit toward other people.

We are constantly enveloped by our human relationships. From womb to grave, ceaselessly, they touch our lives. They are both more immediately and more concretely accessible to us than is God in our day-to-day activities. With rare exception, they occupy a far larger space of time in what we think, feel and do than does God. They are, in short, a much wider "seeding ground" for the practice of vice, and the confession of contrition that should be its result. It is the "flesh," as ancient theologians taught, that is indeed the primary source of our sin—*if* we understand the word "flesh" to mean simply those embodied persons with whom we live and relate: our child, our spouse, our colleague, our neighbor down the street.

Now it may happen, of course, that an individual does indeed commit a specific sin before God that does not directly, even indirectly, touch upon other human beings. We may, for example, curse or deny or mock God. We may, to use metaphors, spit in God's face or turn our back on God. In these cases it is clear that our contrition must also be specifically enacted toward God. It does not involve other people. In fact, they will likely know nothing of our sin before God. But *God* knows it, and that makes all the difference. The sin resides in the relationship. Whether or not it is witnessed by others outside this relationship is irrelevant to the fact that the sin has occurred, that we are aware of it, and that we must therefore confess contrition for it. The same situation would occur whenever I alone know the sin I have committed in my relationship to another human person.

As we noted, no accurate comment can be made on how common direct sin against God is. Sin of this kind is almost always committed "in secret"; it is very rarely a public act witnessed by others. God, of course, does not himself reveal it to others. But what is common, and what each of us has quite adequately experienced, is sin committed against other human beings. We ourselves have committed it; and we have all seen it committed, often, too painfully often. It is sin committed directly against our brothers and sisters that most thoroughly surrounds us and demands our contrition.

Personhood and Humility

Most of us, however, probably find it more difficult to confess contrition before other human beings than before God. For despite our personalized images, we always have it finally in mind that God is indeed God; that he is superior to us in being. But there is no such difference between us and our brothers and sisters. We are the peers of one another, none superior in being to the rest. Our confession to them involves us in submission before others whom we otherwise consider our equals. For in contrition we must yield to the pardon of the other person against whom we have sinned; we must confess to that person the unworthiness of our thoughts, feelings or deeds and ask forgiveness. What this does, of course, is place us in immediate conflict with that "demon" or "spirit" within us that goes by the age-heavy name of pride. It is an easily recognizable demon or spirit—what in the next chapter we will describe more thoroughly in terms like "self-assertion," "self-sufficiency," "autonomy." It is the source of the rebelliousness that can arise whenever we must recognize our dependence on another human being: dependence on his wealth, for example, or his power, or his greater knowledge—or his forgiveness.

What contrition calls for, however, is the opposite of this demon or spirit, its antithesis that goes by the age-heavy name of humility. Humility is the foremost virtue (or attitude) required by contrition. For contrition itself requires an awareness that we are dependent not only on God, but on our brothers and sisters—dependent on their word forgiving our sin, and their word accepting our intended amendment of it. Humility is what allows this awareness; it permits us to go before God, even more so other people, and confess both our failure to live by virtue instead of vice and our intention to rectify this failure. It is what I would call a "heroic" attitude. By it we over-come our powerful reluctance to submit to other human beings. By it we admit to them, first, that we need some-thing from them that we lack; secondly, that this lack is wholly our own responsibility. In our specific context we submit to them in contrition (that is, with regret and the desire to amend) because we recognize our need for their pardon due to a wrong we have freely committed against them. Humility provides the attitude of selflessness requisite for this process; without it, contrition could not be under-taken.

Avoiding Abstraction

It is clear, I think, that we have now passed from our initial reflections, where the "I" was the center of attention in confessing contrition, to a point where the other, the one to whom I confess, has become the center. Whereas previously our interest was in the individual who has com-mitted wrong, our interest now is in the other who has been wronged. We have moved from reflection centered on our own selves to reflection centered on other selves. We have switched our priority, in short, from the subject to the object of our confession of contrition. Our concern is more with the person who has suffered hurt than with the person who has caused it.

Of course, the warning is obvious: The "I" must still be kept conscious; it must not be allowed to slip away. We must always remain aware that it is "I" who have sinned, not some abstract, impersonal "one," or some plural "we." Otherwise how could I take my contrition with the proper seriousness, my sorrow for the sin I have committed and my desire to amend it? Even while concentrating on the wrong itself, or on the person wronged, I must still remain aware of myself.

This concentration on the person wronged also prevents us from falling prey to another type of abstraction. It is what I would call, following the existentialists, the abstraction of the "they," the anonymous crowd. When the others against whom I have sinned are understood in this fashion, contrition again becomes meaningless. For the abstraction has taken away the concreteness of the persons I have failed; "they" have become an empty pronoun.

This is the type of abstraction, for example, that frequently takes place when the wealthy or middle-class reflect on the hungry and poor of the world. These living men, women and children become a "they," a large mass deprived of immediate personal qualities. They are held at a distance; psychologically and socially there is little if any involvement with them as breathing, hurting people. Seldom seen and rarely imagined are their hovels and tattered rags and swollen bellies, their uncared-for wounds and diseased flesh. The result is that any urgency of concern for them is obscured or lost, even while concern for the issues of hunger and poverty might remain. This concern for issues, "topics" divested of their concrete human referents, describes what I mean by abstraction.

Thus I might say: "I have failed so many people. I have hurt them, offended them, disgraced them. My unkindness to them is a cross upon my conscience. Can I ever be forgiven what I have thought, felt and done in their regard?" These statements have a peculiar double quality. They are no doubt sincere and indicate true sorrow; yet they are nameless, anonymous as to the failed others. For whom exactly, then, am I sorrowing over: the one offended, or myself—that I could do such things? The impersonality with which I have collected all those whom I have failed in the words "they" and "them" raises the question: To whom am I confessing my contrition? To myself, perhaps as a type of therapy? If so, then whatever I may be confessing, it is certainly not contrition. For contrition is not only fundamentally but always other-oriented; it is always directed toward the specific, concrete individual whom I have wronged. Its first purpose is always to secure the well-being of this individual, through expressing regret for the wrong committed and the desire to amend it. Only secondarily might it also serve as a palliative for my own conscience, or a source of self-knowledge.

I think it is wise, then, that when expressing contrition formulations of Christian prayer frequently address themselves to "my brothers and sisters." The word "my" is important here. For it not only establishes a relationship with those I have failed; it establishes an intimate, possessive relationship. I am closely bound to the persons I have wronged; they are not "out there," but involved with me. In fact, the word even implies that they are a part of me. When I have hurt and failed them, therefore, I have in a sense hurt and failed myself. In my contrition a sympathetic bond has been established, captured in the word "my," that unites me to those I have wronged. It causes me, for example, to suffer because I have caused suffering, to be ashamed because I have caused shame, to be sorrowful because I have caused sorrow. It brings alive the conviction that in sinning against others I have also sinned against myself; and that in promising amendment to them I am also promising amendment to myself.

The words "brothers and sisters" have a similar effect. Between brothers and sisters there is bond that does not otherwise exist between human beings. It is the bond of a common parentage, a common source, that creates between them a closely felt relationship. To confess to one's "brothers and sisters," then, would again prohibit the others whom I have failed from slipping into a gray anonymity. Their place, instead, would be that of others with whom I am allied, concrete individuals rather than a nameless mass, a "they." Thus we are offered by these words not only a further indication of the personal bond established by the word "my," but a further preventative against abstracting the object of contrition. They create a sense of union with the persons we have wronged that other words, another phrase, might not. A much different frame of mind, for example, would obviously be formed if we were to confess our contrition impersonally, say, "to all concerned" or "to those involved."

The Parenthood of God

As already noted, a phrase like "my brothers and sisters" is clearly meant to describe more than mere consanguinity between individuals, the biological blood relationship that accrues from having a common mother and father. This point has been sufficiently made in the above paragraphs. For what the phrase specifically intends, however, we might do well to return to some remarks made in the previous section about our contrition before God. There we said that because God is the source and sustainer of our life, we must confess contrition to him whenever we have devoted this life to vice rather than virtue. Because we have committed wrong with the life given us, we must involve its giver in our regret and desire to amend. We proposed by this a not-too-fuzzy-headed or complex analysis of the relationship between ourselves and God that initially forms the basis for our confession to him. Our position throughout rested on the rather stark and single assertion in faith that our life finds its final source not in ourselves but in another, and that to this other we are always responsible for what our life involves. This has been the basic idea, the rubric, if you will, for understanding why we confess our contrition to God.

But if I confess my contrition to God because he is the source and sustainer of *my* life, must I not also broaden this idea so as to include *all* lives? If the answer to this question is yes—as I think it must be—then I believe we have the basis for calling all other persons our "brothers and sisters." It is in the one who gives and sustains all our lives that we have our relationship to one another; it is in the realization of this mutual dependence upon God that we all become brothers and sisters to one another.

God is the common ground between us, the "parentage" from which we all derive. He is the source, the cause, the "Father" of that unity that brings us together as children related one to another, brothers and sisters in a mutual heritage. Without such faith in God the question of our communality, of our mutual heritage, must inevitably be reduced to genetics or cultural anthropology, our role as biological or social organisms.

We must strive to make the above faith a working one; we must seek to make it an effective presence in how we act and how we relate to other persons. For it provides the key toward understanding the meaning of our confession of contrition to one another. Without it, I think, we are left hard pressed to see such confession as expressing much more than a pious, uncommitted sentimentality: a putting into words of an attitude, contrition, the individual need not seriously possess. If I do not make my own a faith in God wherein the commonness between myself and other persons is found, my calling them "brothers and sisters" in contrition can too easily become just an empty nicety, a turn of phrase without effect. But it then mocks a relationship that is otherwise meant to be taken with the utmost seriousness. It then pulls the sting from the thought that in offending my brothers and sisters I may also be offending God as well, the common parent of us all.

II.
What Do We Confess in Contrition?

If asked to recapitulate the major theme underlying our reflections in the previous chapter, I would put it as follows: It is I who have sinned, and the sin is my own doing. I cannot place the burden on anyone else's shoulders. I cannot make circumstances the blame for what I have done. I cannot plead family life, social upbringing, lack of education, and so on for the sin that is mine. I must stand before it alone, confessing my responsibility to those I have wronged.

And so it is, I think, that here, with this awareness, confession of contrition begins to become difficult, to sting. For until now we have only named but not discussed what it is we are confessing, and why we are contrite for it. These issues have been floating under the surface all along, to be sure; and we have presumed them throughout the previous chapter. But only now will we bring them into clear relief, into words. *What we are confessing is that we have sinned; why we are contrite is because we have sinned through our own fault.*

I am confessing *sin;* I have sinned. I do not say, "I have made a mistake"; "I have blundered"; "I have not lived up to expectations." I say much more exactly, "I have sinned." What is this sin that we confess with contrition? How might it be viewed and described? It is time to confront these questions directly. From their implied place in the previous chapter we must now bring them center stage. We need to offer some accounting, however brief and straightforward, of what sin means when we speak of "confessing sin" and "being contrite for sin."*

---

1. The Character of Sin

"Sin," as we said in chapter one, is the term I use to describe my specific thoughts, feelings and deeds when they demonstrate vice rather than virtue. It is a term indicating judgment, the judgment that I have thought, felt or done wrongly.

Before this judgment can be made, however, some criterion must clearly be established in order to put a "handle" on what constitutes sin. This criterion will form the background or rubric whereby I can assess the virtue or vice, the right or wrong, in what I have thought, felt and done. Without it, the term "sin" will have either no meaning at all—it is used without a referent; or too versatile a meaning—it is used without discretion.

I would like to suggest that this basis or criterion for what constitutes sin has already been offered in our previous reflections on humility: The basis of sin is to be found in excessive self-assertion. I am in the arena of sin whenever I habitually prefer myself to my brothers and sisters; whenever I put interest in my own self inerrantly

---

* For a more detailed exegetical study of sin than I will give here, see my article, "Sin and Guilt," *Ampleforth Journal*, vol. LXXXI, No. 1 (Spring, 1976), pp. 19-28.

before interest in your self; whenever I unhesitatingly select self-concern over concern for you. This criterion is general, and it is meant to be. A particular sin is not enacted until I put into specific practice my self-concern. That is why we said above that self-concern is only the "arena" of sin; it is not itself sin but the confine within which the *possibility* of sin arises.

It is not without good reason that I have suggested this basis for sin in self-concern. It forms one of the elemental motifs of the teachings of Jesus, and so of the finest traditions of Christian spirituality. We find it, for example, underscoring the Sermon on the Mount, the injunctions of the Kingdom at the end of Matthew's Gospel, and Jesus' unrelenting criticism of the scribes and Pharisees. In each instance self-concern is presented as the source of the wrong, the sin that plagues our existence and makes us unholy before the eyes of God.

But if this is so, then only within the context of a *lack* of self-concern can we adequately understand the meaning of contrition. If the source from which sin emerges is indeed self-centeredness, then contrition can emerge only from a change away from this self-centeredness toward a centeredness on others. If the sin I commit out of self-concern is directed toward others, then my contrition for this sin—my sorrow over it and desire to amend it—must also be directed toward them. And should this sin have been an "open" one, a public sin of which others are aware, then so must the contrition. If in conversation with others, for example, I damage someone's reputation through slander or deceit, contrition requires that I approach them again to rectify this damage. The inappropriateness of following a public sin by a private contrition is obvious enough to allay any further discussion.

A brief digression might now be in order. It regards a clarification of the repeated manner in which we have described the second component of contrition as the desire to amend the wrong we have committed. By the words "desire to amend" I mean to imply more than just a wish or longing to amend. What I have in mind, rather, is a desire that is strong enough to traverse the gap from mere wishing or longing to *promising*. I mean a desire so thoroughly and keenly felt that I become committed to it. I intend to *effect* it, in other words, to actualize it, just as I intend to effect and actualize any promise I might make. If we accept this clarification—brief as it may be—then in what follows the reader will be able to interchange, as I will sometimes do, the phrases "desire to amend" and "promise to amend."

To return to the main flow of our reflections: Only as I realize that sin is the result of an inflated self-concern can I profess adequate contrition. Only as I give up this self-concern in concern for those I have wronged can I begin to regret and desire to amend the sin I have committed. The more I become other-oriented, in short, the more I lessen the seduction to "fall into" sin. But there is pain here; and it cannot be bypassed. It is the pain of realizing that no matter how hard I try, I can never be completely other-oriented—that I will, however much I strive to prevent it, still fall prey to sin and the self-concern that makes it possible. This is the truth contained in the statement, "no man is completely good," and in the doctrine of "original sin." We always live within the ambience of sin because of the self-concern that marks our existence. The task of contrition is to lessen its influence in whatever way, to whatever degree we can.

Yet the truth still remains: The task never ends. A point is never reached when self-concern dissolves completely into concern for others. The task can approximate its goal, moving ever closer to it. But the goal can never be finally gained or fully possessed, like the prize at the end of a race. The self-concern from which sin may emerge is always with us.

As already noted, I have not selected this working description of the basis of sin without good reason. Any brief look at the sources of Christian spirituality finds it readily employed. Everywhere the idea is indicated that sin is born of pride, autonomy, self-seeking; that the ability to sin emerges whenever the individual consistently places concern for self over concern for others. Sin springs from a distorted narcissism, in other words, as the bias toward always valuing oneself above others. And the possibility of this distortion is not something that is realized once or twice or many times in life, and then is gone forever. No, it is not passing, but inherent; it is a constituent part of our selfhood; it is a possibility woven into the very definition of human consciousness.

On this last point, too, we need not confine ourselves solely to the sources of Christian spirituality (scriptures, the Fathers, the manuals of medieval and modern times, and so on). It repeatedly appears as well throughout the best work being done in contemporary psychology. I am thinking, for example, of Norman Brown's fine study, *Life Against Death,* and the doubly fine study by Ernst Becker, *The Denial of Death.* Here also narcissism is presented as a constituent part of the individual, an irreducible element in his personality. The task of every human being is to integrate this narcissism into his life in such a way that it serves virtue rather than vice, according to the value ideals he affirms.

The Example of Narcissus

For a fuller understanding of its meaning, we might do well now to consider at some length the source from which this word "narcissism" derives. This procedure will also provide us with a fuller appreciation of why we said that sin emerges from excessive self-concern, and why this sin should issue in contrition. In all this, of course, we will be clearly emphasizing the "darker" side of narcissism, its role as the milieu in which sin traverses the gap from being a possibility to being enacted. I make this particular point because I am not unaware that narcissism also has a positive aspect: To the degree that any individual is self-involved in what he is becoming, he is narcissistic. In this sense it is an expected quality of human consciousness, and we will examine it at greater length in the next chapter. For the present, however, we are concerned with narcissism, or self-concern, only as the ambience out of which sin emerges—when narcissism, as we have been saying, is "excessive" or "habitual" or "distorted." It will be important to remember this in what follows.

The word "narcissism" derives from Narcissus, the name given the youth in Ovid's famous myth. Narcissus is born beautiful beyond telling, and as he matures he becomes a rival in demeanor even to the greatest gods. He is beloved by all, the object of their constant gaze and attention. Wherever he walks conversation ceases, so pleasant is he to behold. His effect is mesmerizing; others would willingly do anything for him, should he but ask. For his will and intentions are presumed to be good, so divine-like is his beauty. The prejudice of all is in his favor.

The figure of Narcissus, therefore, while the product of mythic imagination, is not completely unfamiliar to us. Each of us has likely met someone with a beauty like his, whose beauty taps feelings from us which other, less beautiful people do not. The history of literature (fictional and true) is also filled with this theme. Think, for example, of Helen of Troy or Dante's Beatrice or the Lady of Shakespeare's sonnets. Here beauty catalyzes a response that an individual would otherwise not make, namely, unguarded rapture with another person, an often blind willingness to do his or her bidding.

But there is a worm at the core of Narcissus—and we must discover it. It does not lie, of course, in his consciousness of his beauty, his knowledge that he is godlike in demeanor. For Narcissus cannot be justly faulted for an appearance that was not his to control. It was a grace, a gift from the gods. But perhaps not precisely that either, when we are thinking soberly. It was more like a *decree* of the gods over which Narcissus had utterly no choice. For he could not refuse his beauty, as he might refuse a true gift. It was there, a part of him, born with him. He was no more responsible for his beauty, and the initial response it drew from others, than he would have been were he born clubfooted or cleft-lipped. Short of a willful, blind obstinacy, he could only affirm of himself what he heard all others say.

No, the worm at the core of Narcissus lies neither in his beauty nor in his recognition of it. It lies, rather, in the *attitude* that this beauty engenders in him; it lies in what the knowledge of his beauty does to Narcissus. This knowledge makes him proud, arrogant, self-infatuated: as the Greek dramatists would say, "overweening." His beauty becomes like a weapon in his hands, with which he uses and abuses others. He comes to delight in the power that he can exercise over others; the way this allows him to bend them to his will. And he delights in the freedom with which he can afterwards shed them from his life, scorning any further relationship. He has had his way with them— whatever it might have involved—and this is all that matters to Narcissus.

That he is wrong in his behavior, of course, never even enters his mind; that he should regret and amend his ways is something he has never thought. He is too content

with the way things are, too satisfied with himself, to consider a change in attitude. The fate which gave him his
beauty gave him power over others. He believes it his
right, even his obligation, to put this power to the service
of his self-concern. It never dawns on him to employ it in
the service of others. The saying of Jesus, "I have not come
to be served, but to serve," would have been greeted by
Narcissus with incomprehension, or gales of laughter.

The gods of Narcissus, however, see his situation much
differently. They are the gods of the Greco-Roman pan-
theon, swift to anger at any human pride, and quick to pun-
ish according to the offense. They are ingenious in dealing
with Narcissus. Enticing him one day to the edge of a still
pool, his eyes fall upon his reflection in the water. And
yes, in an instant he sees there what all others have seen
in him, his irresistible beauty. Like all others he is mes-
merized, riveted by the sight. He cannot take his eyes off
the reflection; he is immobilized. Kneeling there, by the
side of that pool, all he wants to do is gaze upon his beauty,
to feed on it with his eyes. In those moments, nothing else
matters to him. His whole world exists in the image before
him: all it holds of what others have said of him. For in
that mirror of water their words are no longer merely words,
but are confirmed by reality. He sees for himself that he
is indeed the most beautiful of men, a rival, even superior,
to the gods.

But then the tragedy begins to unfold. To be sure,
Narcissus is at first delighted; as we said, he could spend
all his time kneeling there before the pool. After a while,
however, he begins to tire. The image that first enraptured
him begins to lose its drawing power, and his contemplation
of it becomes less and less satisfying. In fact, it soon becomes painful. And the pain is in the realization that in
kneeling there by the pool, unable to move, Narcissus has
lost control of himself, his life. He has become, like Lot's

wife, a pillar of salt, frozen in a vision of himself, and completely unable to dissolve the meaninglessness that he now experiences. Kneeling by that pool, Narcissus deserves our pity. He has looked into his self-infatuation, his too self-centered vision of life, and seen its barrenness. But too late, much too late, for his fate is already decreed, and his gods give no ear to a last-minute repentance. Still breathing, still thinking, still speaking, Narcissus has already returned to the ashes from whence he came, the deadness of a life deprived of a sense of purpose.

Narcissus, of course, represents an extreme case, an "ideal" case if you will, of what happens to any individual overwhelmed with self-concern. He is an exemplar of the paralyzing effect of sin at its extreme—when the individual, so oriented upon himself, is unable to confess his contrition, make amends, and start life anew. His life consequently becomes emptied of meaning. Yet, unwilling to admit that the responsibility for this is his own, he will blame his gods for it, or other people, or even no one. But never does he blame himself, until it is too late. Contrition would have saved Narcissus; but he knows nothing of its meaning. He does indeed deserve our pity—not because of his brutal gods, however, whom we can dismiss, but because of what he is: blind unto death to the sin within him.

Awareness of Sin, Awareness of Place

I have dwelled on the figure of Narcissus at some length because I believe he teaches us much about the nature of sin; what it means to confess sin and intend by this confession regret and the desire to amend. He is the type of individual to whom the statement of Jesus is most clearly directed: Anyone who would save his life (his self) must lose it, and anyone who loses his life (his self) "for my sake" will save it.

But Narcissus asserts just the opposite of Jesus: that the self is saved not by losing it, but by extolling it, by making it the very matrix around which all else revolves. Thus, whatever pertains to this "salvation" of one's self—whatever helps secure the realization of one's desires and designs for one's self—is in the mind of Narcissus justified. Whereas for Jesus excessive self-concern is the ambiance in which sin thrives, for Narcissus it is the ambiance of a successful life. Whereas for Jesus concern for others is a final good in itself, for Narcissus it is only a possible means toward self-aggrandizement.

What Narcissus cannot do, therefore, and any individual like him, is say to another, "I confess with contrition that I have wronged you." The narcissistic individual always has reasons exonerating the wrong he commits, and so feels no need for contrition. Always able to justify what he has done, to give motives for its rightness, the question of wrong is suffocated. It does not even arise.

In this way, of course—by refusing to admit, or by being unaware of the wrong within him and the wrong he does—the narcissistic individual sees no need for amendment. For why should he strive to aright what he does not think is wrong in the first place? Why should he listen to those who condemn what he has become, when it has served so well what he wishes himself to be? Why be contrite for the "good life" that is his, even if its price has sometimes been the hurt of others? "Every man for himself": This ugly warning of imminent danger is willingly embraced as the even uglier motto of every Narcissus.

The difference, therefore, between the narcissistic, self-concerned "I," and the "I" that confesses contrition is finally reduced to the issue of responsibility. And this responsibility, I would say, is twofold. First, it entails the awareness that I am indeed a self-concerned individual, and that I am responsible for the wrong committed against others into which this self-concern has led me. It is the responsibility to keep my eyes wide open, especially when they are inwardly directed at my reasons and motives for thinking, feeling and doing. It is the responsibility that prevents my self-concern from slipping across the line into habitual self-justification. It is the responsibility that forbids a pattern of thought in which the words, *"I have sinned by my own will,"* have no meaning. It is the responsibility which recognizes that just as I am good of my own accord, so am I evil; that I can be willfully wrong-minded, just as I can be willfully right-minded; that just as my virtue is my own doing, so is my vice. It is the responsibility, finally, which from the beginning of human consciousness men and women have too willingly shunned. What, after all, does the book of Genesis understand as the first sin of our ancestors, the couple called Adam and Eve? It is this: that when confronted by God with their disobedience, they make excuses. They blame each other for the wrong each has committed—Adam blames Eve, and Eve blames the serpent; the serpent, conveniently, has no one to blame. What merits God's anger is not so much their act of disobedience as the refusal of the man and woman to take responsibility for it.

Secondly, this responsibility entails what I would call an "awareness of place." By this I mean that despite our self-concern, the importance we attach to ourselves and our lives, we are only *one* person. We are just one of countless others, in a universe of countless worlds. Our responsibility is to make this awareness a personal one; to make it an effective consciousness and not just an unproductive fancy. For with this awareness our self-concern must surely diminish. As we give way more and more to the realization that there are other persons, other worlds, beyond our own individual selves, we realize at the same time that our self-concern has become, not exactly pathetic, but comical.

Let us conclude this section, then, by offering this brief interpretation. Let us say that had Narcissus but for a moment turned his gaze from the pool toward the heavens he would have realized at once his immense insignificance and perhaps been saved from his fate. For the stars would have outstripped him in beauty, and their magnitude would have obliterated his sense of self-importance. They would have taught him humility and powerlessness, that strange serenity which comes from knowing that creation would be as wondrous had he never existed, and that his existence is therefore a blessing. Untouched, unmoved, unscarred by human life, the sky gives wonder and humor to human life. And only Narcissus, or anyone like him, cannot respond in gratitude. And so he dies, made isolated and humorless by his self-concern. Alone, he cannot see beneath his self-concern, into himself, and laugh; nor beyond it, into the heavens, the world of other persons, and be thankful.

2. The Expression of Sin: Thinking, Feeling and Speaking

Throughout the previous reflections we have repeatedly remarked that sin is to be found in how one thinks, feels and acts. We are now ready to specify our reflections in this section, and the two following it, around these three "modes" of sin. Our particular concern in this section will be with the first two of these three modes. Or, if we put it in the form of a question: How might sin be understood regarding the way one thinks and feels? I have combined these two modes, thinking and feeling, for the simple reason that treating them separately would involve us in complex distinctions of human psychology that would serve little purpose here. Instead, I will approach both these modes as essentially a single phenomenon in which precedence will be given to thinking. For it is hard to imagine feelings that do not have, to whatever degree of awareness, a pattern of thought—values, hopes, beliefs—underlying them. We will speak, then, of sinning in thought, all the while recognizing the interwoven, always intricate relationship between thought and feeling.

Self-Concern and Fault

The reflections in the previous section relate directly to the above question—how one sins in thought—and give us its initial answer. An individual is able to sin in thought whenever his thinking is habitually centered on himself, to the harm or exclusion of others. A pattern of thinking that is consistently self-oriented and ego-absorbed is faulty, by which I mean capable of sin. The sin, if we were correct in the last section, emerges from the narrowness of mind that permits us to consider nothing of importance that does not serve our own needs and desires or conduce to fulfilling a certain image we have of ourselves. The ambiance of sin is produced whenever thought is chronically characterized by self-concern.

The above description will provide our "handle" on interpreting what it means to confess that we have sinned in our thoughts. It will be the guide for our contention that sin first takes place within the individual (in his mind, his "heart") before it is expressed outwardly in actions. We must first turn to the way the individual thinks, in other words, before we can adequately understand the sin he enacts.

Before proceeding any further, we might do well to examine at greater length a clarification made in chapter one. We said there that whenever "fault" is used in a context like that above, we are not as yet imputing culpability; that is, we are not as yet making a judgment as to whether or not the individual in "fault" is guilty of committing "sin."

According to our intended usage, rather, the term is a neutral one, employed only to describe a certain dimension of our existence. Any judgment of wrong or evil is thus dependent on a determination of *how* this dimension is enacted in specific instances of day-to-day living. Therefore, to say that self-concern is the basis of fault is not to say that self-concern is itself evil or wrong. It is, as we put it, only the milieu, when excessively engaged, from which wrong or evil emerges—the inclination, the frame of mind out of which wrong or evil is born. Or if we may borrow a term from biological science, self-concern is the "culture" in which wrong or evil can be produced, without itself being wrong or evil. I have repeated this distinction here, and will again draw attention to it, because it serves a key function throughout these reflections, and so must be kept clearly in mind.

Thus it would never do to consider the self-concern of the infant (a la St. Augustine, for example) to be wrong or evil. The infant is committing no wrong when he bites or scratches his mother; or when his screaming demands to be fed keep the mother from her rest; or when he insists on the attention of being held or patted. He does not sin, cannot sin, simply because there is no clear option open to the infant other than his self-interest. His awareness at this stage of life is severely truncated, limited, bounded by the world of his body-consciousness and its demands—the normal, expected responses of the healthy infant.

Yet *fault* is already there, even in the infant. In his screaming demands, his obtuseness and stubbornness in effecting his will, we already see the character of self-concern that every human being carries with him from the first few weeks after birth. We are born selfless, to be sure, unaware of an "I" that sets us apart from our surrounding world. But quickly, within a very short time, we are born again, aware of our self-centered identity. And with this new birth, the beginning of an ego-consciousness, we enter the ambiance of sin. For even though consciousness must yet mature greatly before we can actually commit sin, freely and deliberately, from this point forward sin has nonetheless become a *possibility*. It lurks within us, in our self-concern, until it can be expressed in specific thoughts, feelings and deeds that are wrong yet freely engaged.

Whenever our thinking, therefore, is characterized by self-concern, this fact *of itself* expresses only the condition of our fault, or as some would say, our fallenness. We have not yet committed sin, a moral wrong or evil. Sin enters only when our self-concern specifies itself in certain ways; when our thoughts (and with them, our feelings) take on a particular complexion. This, for example, appears to be one interpretation of the saying of Jesus regarding adultery: "You have heard it said, 'you shall not commit adultery.' But I say to you that anyone who looks at a woman lustfully has already committed adultery with her in his heart" (Mt 5: 27-28). By these words, I would say, Jesus means that sin may express itself not only outwardly, in particular words and deeds, but also inwardly, in a pattern of thought that may or may not be concretely enacted. The importance of this distinction should be stressed because it is too often assumed that sin is confined to doing; that our patterns of thought are free and not susceptible to judgment; that sin can consequently occur only as these patterns are expressed in specific wrong deeds.

If in envy of someone, for example, we think of ways to discredit or ruin his or her reputation, we have in our thoughts already fallen prey to sin. Or if in greed we think of ways to deprive our employees of their just benefits, we have in our thoughts already fallen prey to sin. Or if from spite we think of ways to hurt our spouse, we have in our thoughts already fallen prey to sin. In all these instances—envy, greed and spite—we have specified our self-concerned thinking in ways consistently directed toward the detriment of others. By doing so we have sinned; for the intention of our thought is to harm and in some fashion damage the lives of others. Whether or not we actually express our envy, greed or spite in the ways we have thought is therefore subsequent to the sin involved in first thinking of them. If it happens that we do actually express these thoughts, then the sin is obviously compounded. But if we do not, the sin we have already committed in our thoughts is not thereby eradicated.

Witnesses to Our Thoughts

Of course, in all cases like the above, judgment must initially be made by the individual involved. None of us, unless we are invited, can enter another's thoughts and make the judgment for that person. For while what an individual *does* is open to the judgment of others, what he *thinks* takes place secretly, in his mind, his "heart." It is only when this secret is made public, either in the words voiced or the deeds enacted, that assessment by others becomes possible. Otherwise any assessment can be made, like the thought itself, only in secret, within and by the individual himself. He must himself decide whether a pattern of thought has demonstrated virtue or vice; whether it has been right- or wrong-minded. I say "pattern of thought" here and elsewhere quite intentionally. I am not talking about the random thought that flashes quickly into our minds— "I'd like to kill him"; "I'd like to destroy his reputation"— and then is forgotten. These are largely uncontrollable, emotive responses to passing situations; and it would be inappropriate to find sin in them. No, I am talking about the consistent pursuit of a particular line of thought; the deliberate, conscientious rehearsing of the wrong we would commit against another. I am talking about the thought that has come to be at home in our minds; or perhaps better said, the thought that festers in our minds.

Now the fact that this pattern of thought occurs privately within the individual, "in secret," does not necessarily imply that he alone knows it. Or more precisely, the fact implies only that other human persons do not know it. Because here, I think, we must take into account that blunt, somewhat disturbing assertion Jesus makes about "God who sees in secret" (Mt 6:6). If in faith we abide by this saying, without attempting to dull its bluntness, if we believe that God is indeed a witness to our thoughts, then God too is able to judge them. But even so, the judgment that our thought has slipped from self-concern into sin is in one sense still made in secret. For God, witnessing the sin, announces it to no one. Unlike most of us, God never publicizes the sin within others; he never divulges the vice within their minds and hearts, the wrong they have there committed. Rather, God's witness exists only for the sinning individual. Others can become aware of it only if the individual himself confides it to them.

Let us say, then, that any confession of sin in our thoughts would not ordinarily involve other persons. It would ordinarily be a private confession, a confession "in conscience," made by the sinning individual to God. And furthermore, since the individual alone is aware of private thoughts, and since these thoughts, until enacted in word or deed, do not affect other persons, the regret and promise of amendment would ordinarily also be private. No one else, save God, has been aware of the thoughts; no one else, save God, need witness the contrition.

The sin that has been committed in secret, therefore, in our thoughts, *need* not be shouted from the rooftops, or even quietly confided to a friend. On the other hand, however, it may be: The individual is always free to divulge his thoughts to others. In fact, disclosing to many or just one other person the sin I commit in my thoughts might often be well advised. Sharing with others the sin within me frequently has an ameliorating effect; it consoles, it soothes, it gets the matter "off my chest." But while often advisable, we will not say that such sharing is necessary. Private sin *needs* only private contrition, before God.

Words as Public Acts

But as soon as one goes from confessing sin in thought, to confessing sin in word, the situation changes. Words, as we will understand them, are public; they are meant to be addressed to someone; they are meant to be shared. If we were to speak words when no one could hear them, we might as well have kept silent. Words are intended to be heard or read. Until they are shared in some fashion, they remain thoughts; they remain mine alone.

But once they are voiced or written, once they break the silence of our minds, our thoughts become public acts. Directed now toward others, they are no longer ours alone; other people have become involved in them. And their involvement, though not always affecting them—who is affected by *all* the words he hears?—may at times affect them personally for good or ill. Words spoken in love or sympathy, as we all know, can calm us enormously, more than a caress; words spoken in spite or anger can wound us enormously, more than a physical blow. A poem can console us; a diatribe can make us blind with fury. Our words are *acts;* they may be right- or wrong-minded. They may express virtue or vice; they may damage or heal.

The following is an incident I witnessed a while ago as a slight but concrete example of the ill effect our words might have on others. I was in the company of two men, friends of mine. One, let us call him John, had just completed a project to which he had devoted a great deal of his time, labor and wealth. He had been successful in the task, and was understandably proud of the way it had turned out. He had been talking for quite some time about the various obstacles he had had to overcome, not the least of which was his own recurring desire to give up. With justification he related how he had conquered each of these obstacles in turn, until his project was finally completed. His recitation, I must admit, became a bit too long-winded and precise; he could have spared us many of its details. But out of respect for his accomplishment I remained silent, as did the other man. For I had no wish to dim the full glow of achievement John obviously felt. Not only tact, but my genuine happiness for him constrained any interruption.

When at last he finished, nearly a full hour after he had begun, he looked at each of us with eyes bright and full of satisfied triumph. His joy was transparent; he was a man content with himself and what he had done. I immediately congratulated him, saying how happy I was for him, how pleased that he had completed his task. And I said so easily. My response was born from a respect I did indeed feel for him—one compounded, moreover, by the fact that there had been not a trace of arrogance, no smugness in his recitation. My words were of unqualified praise and admiration; words that I thought he had every reason to hear.

When I had finished speaking, there was a pause. It was clearly meant to be filled by the third partner, and his own words of praise. Yet he said nothing; he only sat there until the pause had gone far enough to become uncomfortable. So I turned to this man, thinking that he might need some prompting, and said, "Well, what do you think? Isn't the completion of John's task something for which he can be proud and take satisfaction?" His response was to look at me and say, with monumental disinterest, "Yes, I guess so"; and then, more animatedly, "Oh, by the way, how about a game of golf tomorrow?" That was all; he stopped speaking and awaited my answer.

The callousness of the man's response, his biting indifference, had their intended effect. For I found out much later that this man was greatly jealous of John's achievement, and the attention it had received. He had therefore made it his purpose, in the course of our meeting, to strike out at John, to wound him as deeply as he could. And he decided, rightly so, that the best way to do this was not to berate or ridicule or find fault with John's deed, but simply to express a total lack of involvement with it: to act as if John had done nothing, or at least nothing of the slightest importance. He succeeded magnificently. John went away from the meeting a damaged and shaken man, his joy and rightful pride dissolved. Those four words, "Yes, I guess so," delivered with such studied disinterest, had hurt him more than any physical blow could have. They paralyzed his mind and heart, his feelings of happiness and satisfaction, and left him a sad and confused man.

The above is just one of countless examples that could be drawn to illustrate the sin we can commit by our words. Out of self-concern we voice sentiments and thoughts that are designed, as in the case of John, to wound or hurt the other, in some fashion to damage his life, or an important part of it. The word that is meant to be constructive or supportive of another person's life is used instead to be destructive and elicit doubts. It demonstrates, in short, an ontological function: It strikes at the individual's very being. It can orient or disorient his life; it can soothe or dismay, unite or estrange, and so on. Our words have power, the power to enact effects, for good or ill, in the one addressed. This is what we recognize when we describe the use of words as "inspiring." To inspire means literally "to breathe into," as when God, for example, is said to breathe life into Adam (cf. Gn 2:7). Words that inspire are words that create—

a frame of mind, a situation, a result. But they may do so not only in the service of virtue, but of vice as well; they may do so to the harm as well as to the healing of others.

Just as our thoughts are private, then, our words are public. They are employed for the sake of the other, to affect him or her in some desired fashion. The judgment made upon them, therefore, must also involve this public dimension. If by our public words, for example, we commit sin, our contrition—our expression of regret and promise of amendment—must also be public. This public may consist of only one: the one to whom we have spoken. Or it may consist of many: a group to whom we have spoken. In either case, however, our contrition must include all those we have wronged by our words. This is the conclusion to be drawn from the position already noted in chapter one, namely, that it is inappropriate for public sin—that is, sin directly involving other persons—to be matched by only a private contrition. For the reigning idea must always be the obvious but often unapplied one: If before others I have sinned, then before them I must also confess my sorrow and promise to amend. In the above case, for example, it would be inappropriate for the man who had offended John to be contrite for his words only in his heart, privately. His confession must also be expressed to the man he has wronged. He would have to go to John and speak his words of sorrow and amendment, just as he had spoken his words of offense. Of course, if it is not possible to do so—if for some reason the person wronged is no longer available— then the obligation is obviously lifted. Being contrite never intends the impossible; the idea is a mockery. A contrite Hitler could never be expected to confess his sorrow and amendment to all those he offended.

Humility and the Amendment of the Mind

As we argued in chapter one, therefore, the task of contrition is truly a task for humility. Contrition always demands some degree of self-abasement—a loss of self in turning toward the others whom I have wronged. It is a task because it is difficult. It requires before the witness of others an abnegation of that self-concern which is so dominant a part of our make-up. In various ways it is to say something like the following: "I consider myself at this moment of less importance than you whom I have wronged"; or, "It is the result that my words have had on you that now matters more than my self-concern, my reluctance to admit that I have committed sin"; or, "It is what I have done to you that is presently more important than my doing it." Each of these statements, and their many variations, indicates the humility necessary to contrition. Each captures the concern for others that in contrition takes precedence over self-concern. Each demonstrates that "swallowing of pride" which allows the individual, first to regret, and then to desire to amend the wrong he has done.

One further point must be made before ending our reflections in this section. Again it is an obvious one, and I would like to put it as follows: The basic amendment that must take place when confessing contrition is always an amendment of thought. This, I would say, is the only conclusion to be drawn from any idea such as, *The sin we fall prey to in our thinking forms the basis of the sin we fall prey to in our words and deeds.* Even in situations when a way of speaking or acting has become habitual—when the individual "automatically" speaks and acts, like Narcissus for example, according to a pattern of self-concerned thought—it is the thought that is transparently at the root of the speaking and acting. It is the thought, therefore, that must first be regretted and amended before the pattern of speaking and acting can be altered. Otherwise contrition tends to become somewhat schizophrenic in its exercise. The individual is placed at odds with himself; conflicts arise between the behavior he desires to manifest outwardly and the inward behavior that describes his thinking and feeling. His words and deeds do not flow from personal conviction.

But contrition, of course, is never meant to induce this type of situation. The sorrow and amendment it demands must flow from a full-hearted, not a halfhearted commitment.

A word can create and a word can destroy. But it is not just God's word that creates and destroys. Our words, too, share in this power. By them we can effect our will, secure a desired result, achieve a wanted purpose. It is a power that draws its motive from within us—from the way we think, the intentions that underlie what we say and do. To amend the wrong we commit, therefore, the sin we enact, is in the first instance to amend how and what we think and feel. The first healing of sin must always take place in the mind, in the heart; only then may our actions also be healed of their sin.

3. **The Expression of Sin: Deeds Committed**

I think we would all agree that responsibility is felt most keenly when it involves the commission or omission of a certain action. An act, a deed, has a concreteness that thoughts do not possess. Thoughts live in a realm of free play, where they can change to a greater or lesser extent with ease. But actions are frozen. Once done they cannot be undone. The individual's responsibility for his actions, therefore, will usually be taken more seriously than his responsibility for his thoughts; he will likely feel freer in thinking than in acting; he will not be as worried by the results of his thinking as of his acting. This same point can be made in a continued variety of ways, but they all boil down to the single idea: To *do* something, to enact a thought in word or deed, implies a greater personal commitment than the thought itself.

In saying this, however, we must still keep in mind what we said at the close of the previous section, where we noted the obvious but often unapplied truth that thinking is the basis for acting. The guide for one's deeds is the intention formed in one's mind. If we allow ourselves to think habitually in a certain fashion, our actions with rare exception will reflect this. If our thoughts are consistently centered around greed or lust, for example, we may fairly expect our actions to be avaricious or promiscuous. A sense of responsibility, in other words, while it may indeed be felt more keenly when involving one's actions, is ultimately of more importance to one's thinking.

The Relation Between Intentions and Deeds

While our sharpest sense of sin arises from what we have done, then, and not from what we have thought, it is from the sin within us, how and what we think, that our deeds emerge. We may entertain for months, for example, the thought of striking someone we dislike. But while the thought never bothered us for a second, or caused even slight remorse, we convict the actual deed itself of sin and express our contrition for it. Yet the deed would likely not have been committed had we not first let its thought fester in our minds.

There is an old saying, dog-eared but to the point, that actions speak louder than words. It means that what matters most is not so much one's motives before acting as the action itself. The saying, of course, is true to the extent that an individual has not in fact done what he intended to do. If despite their desire to raise a good child, for example, the child grows into a liar and thief, the parents' intention does not count for much in passing judgment on how they have in fact raised their child. Or if despite his outspoken misanthropy, an individual habitually gives a large portion of his wealth to the underprivileged, his misanthropic intentions do not matter much in passing judgment on him. In all such cases—and we are each familar with enough of them—what matters most to our judgment is not what is said but what is done. Our judgment is first concerned with the equation between words and deeds, whether or not the intended result is realized.

We will say, therefore, that an intention is fulfilled only as it is enacted in a deed. Otherwise it remains empty; it misses its purpose. But it must still be kept in mind that an intention does not by this fact necessarily remain without sin, as we argued in the previous section. The unrepented intention to harm another, based on envy of him, is already sin; the unredeemed intention not to assist a person in need is already sin. The sin that is committed when and if an intention is actualized in a specific deed is subsequent to the sin that has already been committed in thought. The intention, whatever its result, is itself already sin, because we must take responsibility for how we think as much as for how we act. The relationship between the two, thinking and acting, is indissoluble, and personal accountability spans them both.

In the above examples, then, we cannot excuse our intentions by saying, "I am only thinking of doing this harm; I am only thinking of not assisting this individual in need." An individual cannot dismiss the way he thinks as if it didn't matter. This is especially demonstrated when in other instances the same individual, so quick now to excuse his thinking, will take pride in it as the source of his distinct and praiseworthy achievements. It cannot be important in the one case, when it is a cause for his honor, and unimportant in the next, when it is a cause for his sin. The willingness to take responsibility for the unaided good one does must always be balanced by an equal willingness to take responsibility for the unrepented wrong one does. It is a sure mark of immaturity (or what Ernest Becker calls in a striking phrase, "the characterological lie") when an individual exercises a selective responsibility, taking credit for the virtue in his deeds but ignoring the vice.

The word "unrepented" is used quite deliberately above. It is meant to reintroduce the question of whether or not an intention can cease being sinful if the deed following it is virtuous. We have already touched on this question a few paragraphs ago; now we must examine it at greater length. Despite our intention to harm another out of envy, for example, we praise him instead; despite our intention not to aid another in need, we in fact assist him as much as possible. We have previously argued the obvious sinfulness of an intention when it is followed by the actual deed intended: I intend to ruin this individual's reputation, and in fact I do. We have also argued the (less) obvious sinfulness of an intention when it is followed neither by the actual deed intended, nor by a deed contradicting the intention: I intend to ruin this individual's reputation, but I neither enact nor contradict the intention by my deeds. The question now confronting us, however, is this: Does the deed which contradicts a sinful intention redeem the intention? Or are the intention and deed so autonomous in a given instance that the individual can sin in one and be virtuous in the other?

This is a complex, difficult question, and it has exercised the talents of moral theologians and philosophers for centuries. If I were asked to take a stance on it now, though, I would have to side with those who say that the deed can indeed redeem the intention in any given instance. Thus I would confirm that basic inclination in judgment noted at the beginning of this section: The rightness of the act overrules the wrongness of the intention. I would repeat, however, that if the intention is not followed by such an act—that is, if the individual in fact does what he intends to do, or if he does nothing to contradict his intention—then the intention is still marked by sin. But if the sinful intention is belied by the good deed, then I say the intention is redeemed.

The deed always "proves" what the individual intends; it confirms or denies his resolve. It demonstrates the degree of commitment the individual has attached to intentions, to thoughts; as we said, it provides the criterion for judging them. But when a wicked intention is followed by a good deed, what are we to say except that the intention has somehow been overcome? Perhaps it was never strong enough to be enacted—the individual's inclination away from wickedness proved finally stronger than his intention to commit wrong. Or perhaps at the moment of its execution the individual underwent an instinctual or intuitive alteration of his intention to commit wrong—that sudden phenomenon we have all experienced as a "change of heart."

As a sobering influence we must now add that the above idea is not meant to be applied across the board, but only within the confines of specific situations. The intention and the deed that follows it are to be judged according to the single context in which they take place. The fact that one has intended harm out of envy in one given context, for example, and then tries to excuse it because he has acted unenviously in another context, will just not do. For the question of sin always arises within the context of a given set of circumstances; and it is *there alone* that we must judge whether or not sin has taken place. This has provided a defining and recurring motif throughout the reflections in this book, and to it we now and will again remain faithful. More specifically, it follows as a direct consequence of our previous discussion regarding the distinction between fault and sin: Fault is the condition; sin is the particular enactment of this condition within a given context. Therefore, just as one should not demean present virtue because of past sin, one cannot excuse present sin because of past virtue. Rather, every intended act of virtue, every intended act of vice, must be judged according to its own context. What the individual has done in the past is not pertinent in judging the rightness or wrongness of his present intention and the deed which does or does not follow it.

The Redeemed Intention: An Example

Perhaps an example might help clarify the point we are discussing, as well as introduce an element of concreteness into it.

Let us say there is a woman who from envy of her neighbor's well-behaved and talented children (as compared to her own) intends to start "telling stories" about them designed to discredit their behavior and talent. Let us say that as each day goes by her envy becomes more and more refined; she rehearses over and again what she intends to say. It will not be a frontal, hysterical attack, but a subtle one marked by innuendo and allusion. She does not wish to explode the reputation of the children all at once; her intent would then be too plain. Instead, she wishes to be indirect, to introduce a cancer into their reputation that will slowly eat it away. In this fashion she will "get even" with the fate that has given such good children to her neighbor but not to her. The children have done her no harm, but they are a constant reminder of what she herself does not have. They are a thorn in her mind.

But let us also say that one day this same woman falls ill. She is bedridden and cannot carry out her daily tasks. Her own children are of no use; they refuse to disrupt their plans and activities to help her. This, however, is only to be expected, since she has always tolerated their ego-oriented motives, their willful self-indulgence. Yet days go by, and she is becoming more and more anxious. For she is a fastidious housekeeper, and her home has become dirty, unkempt, and slightly foul-smelling. She wishes there were someone upon whom she could depend to put the place in order and relieve her anxiety. But she can think of no one to whom she can turn; no one upon whom she can place the burden of caring for her needs. She is alone in her illness; and the illness makes her loneliness all the more poignant.

Then one morning the children of her neighbor appear. They offer their good wishes for her quick recovery, and then ask if there is any help she needs. She hesitates—but before she can respond they begin the task of cleaning. They see the need, and go to meet it without delay or further questioning. Within a short while her home is as she likes it, and her anxieties about its unkemptness have disappeared. She offers some payment, but they refuse. When asked why they gave up their time to help her, their response is that she is ill and cannot do it for herself. It is a simple response, to match the simple charity they manifest. She senses no guile in it, no ulterior motive. They are expecting nothing from her: no payment, no praise—not even, she suspects, her gratitude. They are satisfied simply enough with being able to assist her in her need. And again wishing her a quick recovery, they depart. The whole experience was the closest the woman had ever come to innocent virtue, that "purity of heart" of which we spoke in chapter one.

From that day onward, the woman forsakes her intention to discredit these children. Instead, a fondness for them begins growing in her. Instead of demeaning them before others, she now praises them. She publicly admits (confesses) their goodness of heart and generosity; she privately recognizes that these are virtues her own children do not possess. Yet she also recognizes, as we said, that the responsibility for her children's self-centeredness is not entirely theirs, but also hers. She resolves, therefore, to talk to her neighbor, seeking advice on how to make her own children better, less self-concerned persons. From the help given her by her neighbor's children, she has become aware that she needs further help. From that single experience of their generosity, lasting but a short while in time, she has forged a new and determined intention: to learn where she has failed with her own children, and to attempt its correction.

Now what may we say of the woman's original intention? Shouldn't we say that it is redeemed by her subsequent actions? Originally her intention was to damage the reputation of her neighbor's children; to demean them in the eyes of others. But in fact she praises them. Now she even seeks to form her own children into being more like them, expressing a similar generosity and kindheartedness. Her actions, in short, are a direct contradiction of her original intention. We could even say that they express her contrition for this intention, her sorrow and desire to amend it. Can we blame her, then, for what she intended but did not do, for in fact doing just the opposite? In judging her can we give precedence to her one-time resolve, which she never actualized anyway, and ignore her deeds which deny it? Can we condemn her unrealized intention as sin?

To each of these questions I would answer no. Any damage to others she could have done, she did not do. Her first intention remained private, unshared. Even more, while not enacted, it did not remain unchanged; her subsequent behavior demonstrates that it had altered radically. From resolving to harm, she now resolves to commend.

The vice that she first meant to commit she not only does not commit, but replaces with the practice of virtue. The self-concern that initially prompted her envy is replaced by the confession of her mistake in rearing her own children. Her initial arrogance is replaced by humility. In this whole process, I would say, she has adequately expressed her contrition. She has repented her first desire to commit sin and "proved" its redemption in what she actually does.

Now if I were to ask what basis might exist for this interpretation, many readers would no doubt respond correctly: the message of Christ in the gospels. And if I were to ask what particular part of this message, many would no doubt again respond correctly. The basis for my interpretation is the question Jesus poses to his disciples and the answer they affirm in the following words, this striking parable:

> What do you think? A man had two sons; and he went to the first and said, "Son, go and work in the vineyard today." And he answered, "I will not"; but afterward he repented and went. And he went to the second and said the same; and he answered, "I go, sir," but did not go. Which of the two did the will of the father? They said, "The first" (Mt 21:28-31).

The good deed that denies the bad intention is the individual's literal *act* of contrition. By doing good where he previously meant to do wrong, the individual has redeemed his first resolve. In what he actually does he demonstrates not only his regret over his initial intention, but also his desire to amend it. The question, then, should no longer be raised as to whether or not in his first, unrealized resolve he committed sin; for his subsequent actions have already answered it, negatively.

Retribution and Resolution

There is one further point, I believe, that should be drawn from the above parable. We have touched on it before, and it may be simply put as follows: The amendment we promise in contrition cannot be excused. Whatever our sin, we must be willing to demonstrate in some way our desire to rectify it. No sin can be committed for which we cannot to some degree make amends. No matter how fervently we might devote ourselves to a pattern of wrong-doing, no matter how excessively we give reign to our self-concern, we always have before us the option of regret and amendment.

This is not an option, however, that need be *given* us, as if of ourselves we have no power to rectify the wrong we have done. No, it is an option that is always open to us, waiting to be chosen. Thus, the young son in the parable who at first refused his father's request was later able to grant it. The option to do so, until at last he chose it, always remained a possibility for him. His initial refusal did not lock him into a permanent refusal. His initial wrongdoing, his denial of his father's request, was always capable of being rectified.

As we noted in the previous section, though, it may sometimes happen that the individual cannot *completely* amend the wrong he has done—as the young son was able to do in Jesus' parable. In all specific instances he might not be able to rectify fully the harm he has caused other persons, to restore them to what they were before he wronged them. But I would suggest that this issue—that is, the offering of retribution equal to the damage done by the sin committed—enters as only a partial consideration into the question of amendment. It enters, I would say, to the extent that the individual *wants* and *attempts* (given his

limits) to make adequate retribution. If he cannot, however, then I would say but one response remains open,
namely, the persons sinned against must exercise mercy,
forgiving the individual the debt of retribution he cannot
fulfill. For within any Christian life is not the *lex talionis*
("an eye for an eye; a tooth for a tooth") meant to be overcome? Is not the teaching of Jesus clear: When we
are sinned against, our task is to absolve, not to exact an
equal revenge? It is the Old Law that demands utter retribution, and amendment equal to the offense. But the Law
of Christ demands mercy, even a mercy shown seven by
seventy times.

I said above that the issue of retribution enters only
partially into the question of amendment. I think we can
now specify this point even further. I would do so by saying
that the basic interest of retribution is that dimension of
amendment concerned with the present as it relates to the
past. This concern would find expression, for example, in
the questions: What must I *now* do to rectify the particular
wrong I *have* done; how can I now "pay back" in virtue the
vice I have committed? I cannot presently behave as if
nothing had happened; as if the past did not exist. If by
my sin I have deprived another of some good (his reputation, his rightful earnings, his peace of mind, etc.), I must
now somehow satisfy this deprivation. It is a wrong I have
done; it is a wrong I must now attempt to correct. In contrition, therefore, the past is not only remembered. It also
exercises a present influence as the motive for the individual's offering retribution—for his now seeking to aright the
wrong he has done.

Let us add in conclusion, however, that just as amendment does indeed involve this element of the past, so it also
involves the future. The individual must perceive his
amendment as applying not only to what he *has* done, but
to what he *will* do. In other words, insofar as it involves

amendment, contrition requires not only retribution but also resolution. As we will see more fully in the next chapter, it requires that the individual lay hold of his future; that he resolve to guide it away from the vice that has marked his past toward the future practice of virtue. It demands, in short, that the individual change; that he not remain the same, prey to the same sin, but become someone different—someone, I would say, marked by the same change recorded of the young Jesus: "And Jesus increased in wisdom and stature, and in favor with God and man" (Lk 2:52).

4. The Expression of Sin: Deeds Omitted

Just as our reflections in the previous section were concerned with wrongful acts of "commission," our reflections now will be concerned with wrongful acts of "omission." In this section we will reflect on contrition for deeds we should have done, but did not. Just as it is possible out of self-concern to sin in the performance of a particular act, so it is possible out of self-concern to sin in the refusal of a particular act. For, save when its source is ignorance, our failure or refusal to act, our silence, must be construed as the product of a choice. So, within any given situation we do or do not act; we do or do not respond; we do or do not take interest; and so on. To accept responsibility for our actions clearly applies not only to what we have done, but to what we have failed to do.

Distress over Our Failure to Act: An Extreme Case

Some of the most disturbing behavior of human beings falls into the latter category. I am thinking, for example, of newspaper accounts of several years ago relating the incident of a death by stabbing—and the extensive discussions it catalyzed in books and magazines, on radio and television. The stabbing took place in full view of more than 30 people, looking on from windows and around corners. Yet not one of them, not a single one, did anything to assist the woman being murdered. *They just stood there and watched.* Horrified, shocked by the blood and brutality, each gave as a reason: I did not want to get involved.

While we may sympathize with the situation of these people, and the honesty of their response, we must still ask whether their reason is sufficient; is it exonerating? And we must reply: no, not nearly sufficient, not exonerating at all. In omitting any deed to help the woman, each of these onlookers, I would say, fell prey to sin. Their self-concern in this particular instance, their not wanting to "get involved," had traversed the gap from fault to sin. To be sure, had there been but two or three of them, they might have felt this way with justification. Their hopelessness in overcoming the murderers might well have justified their sense of self-preservation. But 30 of them!—could not a large portion or all of them have quickly banded together in a community and done something, anything, to aid the woman? It is hard to believe they could not, despite their individual fears. Yet the truth is that they did not. They refused to act, and in this, I would say, they did wrong.

The above incident should shock anyone with an ounce of moral sense. It is shocking, in fact, in a way that is even more disturbing than the actual crime that took place. For whatever the insane motive for such an act, however base or pathetic, our newspapers, radios and televisions are saturated with similar incidents every day. In our society they have become so commonplace that in our minds we have become accustomed to the bloodlust or greed, the perversions that motivate the murder of human beings. Yet we have not grown accustomed to the fact, we are deeply distressed by the fact, that 30 men and women witnessed such a crime and did not stir. Before this fact our mind is frozen by strangeness—its moral sense stripped and tortured by the question: How could they have done nothing, nothing?

Individuals who pose this question, and are perplexed in seeking its answer, do not give full credit to the degree that self-concern can extend as a motive for acting or not acting. More specifically, they seem unaware, or refuse to acknowledge, the absolute value men and women easily place on their safety, their health, their aversion to pain— how instinctively we all draw back from anything that threatens our well-being; how blind our self-concern can be. The witnesses, after all, were not only repulsed by what they saw; they were terrified by it. The thought kept crossing their minds with each time the woman was stabbed: "If I go to help her, I might also be stabbed, steel into my flesh. My assistance, then, would merit me nothing but terrible injury, or death. Yet here at my window (or around this corner) I am secure. Here I am at a safe distance from the event. So here I will stay." And then without doubt, one further thought also crossed the minds of many: "Why doesn't somebody else help her?"

But everyone else, of course, was thinking fairly much the same thoughts, with many asking fairly much the same question. Each witness knew that only the pathological mind enacts murder; that the balanced, healthy mind does not obey the mad thought of killing other human beings. But each witness also knew that the pathology of murder is often indiscreet: If you get in the murderer's way, if you try to stop him, he will attempt to kill *you*. Each witness knew, therefore, that any proximate involvement with the murdering individuals before him would place his own life in jeopardy. And so, thinking first of themselves, and not thinking of helping one another to help the woman, the witnesses remained inert in their self-concern.

Their sin, therefore, was a sin of omission: not doing what they ought to have done, despite their individual fear and terror. And our distress is greater over them than over the murderers, not only because of their inertia, but because we easily see ourselves in their very same situation and behaving in exactly the same way. Far more frequently than we like to admit, each of us has also omitted the good we should do, the virtue we ought to express.

Judging Our Failures to Act

What is essential to our discussion of the sin of omission is the idea that the omission may be deliberate or indeliberate. An individual may, for example, intentionally or unintentionally omit a name from a guest list he is preparing. The deed may be either a conscious refusal or simply the result of forgetfulness. If the latter is the case, not much more can be said. When neglect is caused by forgetfulness, there is little to be gained from seeking reasons for it. In the following reflections, therefore, we will eschew all interest in omission through forgetfulness and concentrate instead on the former case, omission through conscious refusal.

When an individual consciously refuses to do something, his refusal may be judged in either one of two basic ways. In the first, judgment is neutral. Here the individual may refuse to do something (just as he may agree to do it) without our raising the question of its moral rightness or wrongness. It is simply a matter of amoral preference, and any discussion of its moral rectitude becomes ludicrous. The individual may refuse to go to the country in an automobile, for example, preferring a bicycle instead; or he may refuse to carry an umbrella on an overcast morning, since he prefers not to be encumbered with it; or he may refuse to study Dickens instead of Tolstoy for the coming week; and so on. No one in his right mind would seriously attempt to cast these refusals into categories of moral right and wrong.

But an entirely different situation arises when we come to the second way of judging an act of conscious refusal. Here omission takes on the specific meaning of active or deliberate neglect. By this I mean that in following a certain pattern of activity, the individual is judged to have acted not amorally but immorally: He or she did not do what ought to have been done. Whatever the specific context, the individual's self-concern in refusing to act now brings forward the question of sin.

The key word, of course, is "ought," and I would suggest it contains at least three implications. First, it implies that according to whatever norms are employed, the individual's refusal to act offends these norms. Between doing and not doing something, one freely chooses not to do it, and so is held accountably wrong. Secondly, the word implies that the issue under consideration is of sufficient importance for the individual himself and/or the society in which he lives. In this sense, it would be a misuse of the word to say that someone *ought* to read Tolstoy rather than Dickens, or carry an umbrella on an overcast day. But it would not be a misuse to say that we ought to tell the truth or aid the infirm or care for our children.

The third implication follows from the first two, and brings us once again to the question of responsibility. Sometimes this question is clearly perceived, and can be answered readily. In the incident previously cited, for example, the responsibility of the 30 men and women was clearly to assist the woman being murdered, so that their refusal to do so clearly constitutes a failure in this responsibility. But, even more, because the situation in which their responsibility succumbed to their self-concern was an important one, yet one (had they acted together) not clearly involving anyone's self-destruction, their refusal to act ceased being just an amoral decision and became an immoral one. Whenever a refusal that is consciously intended involves the individual in an option for self-concern (here avoiding the issue of self-preservation) to the harm or hurt of others, we are in the domain of sin. And whenever we deliberately eliminate virtue from the way we behave because it counters our self-concern, without clearly threatening our life, we have committed wrong. Our responsibility for sin, therefore, is always double-edged. It is exercised whenever we do what we ought not to do, and whenever we do not do what we ought to do.

Examples like the above are easy enough to find—they fill our whole lives—and the question of responsibility in them is obvious enough. It is a responsibility directly related to the specific deed involved: not giving aid to a woman being murdered, not giving food to a beggar at your door, not caring for your sick child, etc. But there is another dimension to responsibility that is more oblique, not quite so easily related to particular deeds. I would like to consider it now—first and most obviously, because I think it is important; but secondly because its very indirectness frequently leads to its importance being "cloaked," that is, denied or ignored as having no immediate bearing on the individual's life and activities. I think the best way to proceed would be to give a concrete example of what I mean.

Let us say you are a businessman whose goal is to "reach the top." For years you have devoted your time and energy toward this goal. You work 10 hours a day at the office; and on most nights, invariably on weekends, you bring a portfolio of paperwork home with you. You are compulsive about knowing every facet of your business life, and doing whatever is needed to achieve this. For the thought constantly worries you that another, more talented (or ruthless) man will catch the eye of your employers and take your place in their favor. Your image of yourself "at the top," therefore, and your plans for getting there, demand permanent attention. Your self-concern, that is, your career-success, is always under threat. One wrong decision, one display of ignorance, one personal indiscretion—one serious mistake of any kind and your career could be left a shambles, your self-concern a failure.

Now with your compulsion, of course, your single-minded ambition to succeed in business, you also find that you must habitually omit any prolonged attention to other dimensions of your life. Your children are given over completely to the care of your wife; your wife is expected to take care of herself. You have nothing to do with your neighbors; you do not have the time to spend with them. You have no hobbies and play no sports; they are, you say, too time-consuming. You faithfully study whatever pertains to your business, but outside of that you read only the daily newspaper; never a novel, never poetry, history or science. Even then, you unfold the paper and flip immediately to the business section; only rarely do you read the headline stories, and never the section dealing with art or cultural events. On and on the recital could go. But its conclusion is clear: Your self-concern has set severe limits on your life, tightly binding what you are and likely will be. It has made the world of your interests a small, closed circle, in which you are comfortable and conversant only with career-oriented issues.

You are, to any objective observer, pathetically unaware of what is happening politically, socially, religiously in your society. But that is plainly understandable. You have had to eliminate any involvement with these matters for the sake of your self-concern, your ambition. You are not even completely aware of what is happening in your own family. You only want to be engaged there in what you call the "important" matters, the crises that might disrupt your normal routine if left unattended. But ordinarily when you come home in the evening you only want to be fed, have enough quiet to do your "homework," perhaps watch some television, perhaps have sex with your wife, and then go to sleep. The weekends you expect to be only an extended version of this same routine. Any thought to the contrary—a short vacation with your wife, a day or two of camping with your children, night or weekend courses at the local college—quickly dies in your mind.

It is little wonder, therefore, that when issues like civil rights or religious freedom are raised, you are completely unconcerned with them. They do not matter to you because you have consciously avoided taking any interest in them. The fact that people are dying from lack of food or lack of justice floats around on the periphery of your consciousness, like the question of what you ate for supper last night. You have omitted this fact from your engaged attention, because it is an intruder on the self-concerned ambition to which you have devoted your time and efforts. What would happen to your career, after all, your growing bank account, if you began taking seriously the suffering or injustice inflicted on others, perhaps by your own employers? How could you advance in the business world if your attention were turned toward the hunger and poverty in the Third World? What would your associates think if you began talking too much of underfed children, abused laborers, tortured dissidents, slaughtered missionaries? How would your bosses react if your devotion to your job was not total but shared; what suspicions would they have over your other concerns?

Having omitted from your life, then, any conscientious awareness of facts like civil and religious oppression, you can hardly bring yourself to do anything about them, however small. If people die of hunger or torture or rampant disease, you don't even raise the question: "What can I do to help?" Instead, your question is: "Why doesn't somebody else help them? I can't get involved." But at this point, of course, you are not very far from the same basic attitude of the 30 men and women who did nothing while a woman was being stabbed to death. Your response indicates that something should be done, but that you are not the one to do it. You are aware of the hungry, tortured and diseased, but their plight is shed of any personal application. They are "out there," having nothing to do with your immediate concerns, certainly nothing to do with your career. You are, in fact, about as committed to their plight as you are to the geology of the moon. In no fashion do you understand them to be your "brothers and sisters"—as we described this phrase in chapter one.

Correcting Our Failures to Act

The message of Christ, let us say, is delicately balanced between an encouragement not to commit certain acts and not to omit others. The whole of the 25th chapter in the Gospel of Matthew can be seen as an excellent example of the second side of this balance. Salvation is there secured through the performance of charitable deeds, and lost through their omission. It is not sufficient, it is not redemptive only to avoid the commission of vice; one must also avoid the omission of virtue. The same motif can also be found, though less directly, in St. Matthew's version of the Sermon on the Mount, the eight beatitudes and the promises attached. There too the idea reigns that salvation—a life like Christ's—demands not only that vice be avoided but that virtue not be ignored. As we said, the "saved" life taught by Jesus clearly requires a double-edged activity: of not committing and not omitting certain deeds.

It should now be obvious, therefore, wherein contrition lies when the sin in question is one of omission. It lies in sorrow for not performing the deed that has heretofore been lacking, and in the promise to rectify this lack in the future. If people have intentionally omitted to care for the poor or sick, for example, then their contrition demands that they regret and amend this omission. More generally: If they have omitted from their lives *any* act that virtue demands, their contrition requires that they begin including it. For we cannot merely confess in sorrow that we have omitted virtue in our lives, and then do nothing more, content with our sorrow. Our confession, if it involves contrition, must also be followed by deeds correcting the failure; our sorrow must find expression in what we henceforth do.

In the above paragraph I have intentionally employed the phrase "in our lives"—and so have returned to a repeated theme throughout these reflections. Persons who sin through omission can obviously make amends for this only within the context of their own existence. By this I mean that the amendment is to be carried out in whatever situations their daily lives afford. Or otherwise put: We cannot be fairly expected to alter our life-style radically in pursuit of our amendment. To be sure, such alteration may and sometimes does occur. There are numerous instances of people who have undergone radical changes in external lifestyle in expressing the amendment of sin that they believe their contrition demands. There is always the witness of the saints—an Anthony, for example, a Francis, a Teresa. But the point is that we cannot fairly *expect* such radical conversion, let alone demand it, of ourselves or others. A housewife cannot be expected to enter a disciplined convent to amend her pride, a businessman to enter a silent desert to amend his greed, a teenager to promise eternal celibacy to amend his lust. These are possibilities *in extremis;* even if other responsibilities permitted them, contrition can certainly not require them.

Instead, our amendment will ordinarily take place in the same arena where our sin did: the arena of our present

life-situation. When contexts arise wherein we should practice a virtue we previously neglected, we now do. This is
the willingness that signals contrition when our sin has been
one of omission. When we meet the poor and hungry, we
now clothe and feed them; when we come across someone
needing our understanding, we now give it; when we en-
counter a person who asks our time or help, we now offer
it. The generosity, the humility, the lack of self-concern
that we previously omitted from our thinking and deeds, we
now make living and effective attitudes in our behavior. The
deed we now enact, which previously we did not, is our
literal act of contrition whenever we confess that we have
sinned in what we have failed to do.

III.
For What Do We Ask in Contrition?

While researching for this book the various formulae for contrition scattered throughout Christian tradition, I found a repeated, almost consistent practice of petitioning both the saints and our living brothers and sisters. The petition, in one form or another, centers on a request that these dead and living Christians *pray* for us.* Recognizing this tradition and—as I hope to demonstrate—finding it important and contributive to our understanding of contrition, I will devote the reflections in this chapter to the following three issues: first, to the meaning of the role of the saints in our confession of contrition; secondly, to the meaning of the role of the living in this confession; and thirdly, to the meaning of the specific request that we make of these dead and living Christians, namely, that they pray for us.

---

* See, for example, the formula for contrition employed in the rite of reconciliation initiating the Catholic liturgy of the Eucharist.

1. **Petitioning the Dead**

The meaning of this idea, petitioning the dead, will not become fully clear until we reach the last section of this chapter—where, as we said, we will consider more thoroughly what it is we are requesting. Yet I think it is also important to consider the idea on its own merits, since it specifies for us in ways not yet done the meaning of a properly Christian confession of contrition for sin. This is not to say, of course, that until now we have not been concerned with this Christian dimension. We obviously have. The previous chapters repeatedly make reference to the person and words of Christ. In fact, our principal rubric for understanding the idea of sin, for suggesting that sin arises from self-concern, is a product of reflection on the meaning of Christ's life and words. What the idea, petitioning the dead, does is not to initiate us into an involvement with the Christian understanding of contrition for sin, but to amplify this involvement.

The idea implicitly raises a number of issues (or presuppositions) that are perplexing and difficult, though for that reason no less central to the tradition of Christian faith. A detailed study of them, however, while appropriate to a prolonged study of doctrine, would be quite inappropriate here. We will have to be content, therefore, with only a brief presentation of what I think these issues to be, and how they might be applied to the question of Christian contrition.

Characteristics of Resurrection Life

The first presupposition in the idea of petitioning the dead is that the dead enjoy some form of conscious existence—which is but another, more explicit, way of stating the Christian doctrine of resurrection. This doctrine splits into two parts. First, it involves the question of the resurrection of Jesus: Was Jesus raised from the dead as the New Testament asserts, and does he now enjoy a conscious identity? If we answer this question affirmatively—that is, if we agree that in some fashion Jesus is presently alive—the doctrine then involves the question of whether this resurrection life is available to others. If this question is also answered affirmatively, then the presupposition underlying the idea of petitioning the dead is thereby justified. When we confess contrition to these persons, and in the process seek their assistance, we are assenting to the idea that as Christ lives, so do they. We are not confessing our contrition to a mere memory, in other words, or seeking the aid of dead and rotted corpses: ludicrous ideas both. No, our address is to beings we take to be living and conscious, even if the specifics of their existence are beyond our telling.

The first, and I think most fundamental point to be made about our idea, therefore, is that it assumes some type of conscious existence beyond death. Furthermore, it assumes that this conscious existence is a personal one. For just as we would hardly ask something of the dead were they not presumed to enjoy a conscious existence, neither would we specify by name the ones being asked (e.g., St. Francis, St. Teresa, Mary, etc.) if we did not think they enjoyed a personal existence distinct from others.

It is not just anyone, therefore, to whom we are now confessing our contrition; it is not just anyone of whom we are making a request. Our confession, our request are neither made nor directed anonymously. It is "I" who make them—but not "to anyone who will listen," not "to whom it may concern." Rather, I make them to others who I believe are as personally distinct as I myself am.

It is precisely this personal existence, as we said, that is presumed in the specific address of our confession. What are being shunned by our use of a particular name are all ideas that the consciousness attained after death is not a personal one, or solely a communal one, as if the dead melded into one great mind or a single all-absorbing consciousness. The naming of a saint is meant to express fidelity to the ancient tradition that the dead retain something of the conscious identity they enjoyed during earthly life. But again—in what this specifically consists we cannot say. Does it include doubt or anxiety, or a more direct awareness of the presence and qualities of God? Does it involve an unqualified love, as St. Paul affirms (cf. 1 Cor 13:1-13), or any of the affective emotions such as anger or glee? How are others perceived; what "form" do they take? Are there colors and shapes and movement? Questions like these can be asked forever; they are, I think, the product of a legitimate curiosity. But not one of their answers can be justified by actual experience, defined in unquestionable fashion. To some degree each response remains prey to the uncertainty of imagination.

With regard to confessing contrition, then, the psychological application (at any rate) of our point seems clear enough. For if the dead are thought to be absorbed into a single consciousness, how could we relate to them? More exactly, how could we confess to this single consciousness; how could we identify it? For confession, we have maintained, establishes a relationship between one person and another; it demands personal recognition between them. But doesn't the notion of personhood lose all meaning if after death the individual's consciousness is thought to be subsumed in, lost in its contribution toward, some "cosmic" or "universal" consciousness? How could we possibly address this consciousness; how could we name or recognize or describe it? Clearly, I think, we could not—at least not in any way affectively satisfying for us. What is demanded, rather, is some understanding of life after death that permits our personal involvement, our ability to name and recognize, to relate to the dead. The reader will recall that this is the same fundamental point we were making in chapter one while discussing how the image of God also required us to confess our contrition affectively to him.

We will try to determine shortly just what this personal involvement might include. But for now we may note that to construe it along the lines of a ghostly inhabitation of the world, wherein the dead are understood as unseen presences capable of manipulating our lives, is inadequate. We can give no serious consideration here to the claims made by mediums and spiritualists that the dead can and do speak to them, can and do move objects, can and do alter events, and so on. Nor can we give serious attention here to the claim of many saintly men and women, otherwise known for their realism, that the dead can and do appear to them in perceptible human form. These claims, while perhaps interesting in other contexts, are not germane when discussing the agency of the dead in our confession of contrition. For that agency, I would now suggest, is fundamentally one of the service that their earthly lives can render us in our relationship to God and one another.

We will be discussing the above suggestion at some length in the pages that follow. For now, however, we should note that it leads us into a second observation about the idea of petitioning the dead. It not only presumes that the dead possess personal consciousness, but that they can somehow respond to our petition. It would hardly make sense otherwise to ask something of them. When we confess contrition to the dead, in other words, and seek a response on their part, we are acknowledging that they are not only conscious but responsive beings, in much the same way as when they were alive on earth. Again, can we "prove" the existence of such individuals by direct apprehension? No, we obviously cannot. We cannot see them smile or weep at our contrition, nod at our request.

We cannot point to them in place or embrace them. All we can do is assert that they are conscious and responsive, in these qualities sharing a common humanity with us. But this assertion can always and only be made in faith: what I think St. Paul is doing, for example, in 1 Corinthians 15 when he speaks of the dead as having "spiritual bodies." In some fashion we must understand the dead as being like unto us, or like unto themselves in earthly life (as having a "body"), though also as somehow clearly different from us (theirs is a "spiritual" body).

One further point must also be made about the idea of petitioning the dead as it appears in various formulae (personal or communal) of contrition. The idea implies that we have a certain responsibility toward the dead. For the fact that we ask their prayers indicates, I would think, at least this much responsibility: that we seek their assistance in meeting the demands (proper sorrow and amendment) required by our contrition for sin. In fact, it is precisely this idea that will form the theme for the rest of our reflections in this section.

Dead and Forgotten?

From the above remarks we are obliged to conclude that the saying "dead and forgotten" clearly has no place in Christian contrition. The dead are unmistakably understood as possessing certain shared human qualities that allow for our present involvement with them. The fact that they are addressed in confession, that a request is made of them, would otherwise be reduced to a farcical activity. We cannot ask something of a memory, still less of a rotted corpse, and do so with serious intent. Only if the dead are accepted as somehow still similar to us, as enjoying a conscious and personal existence, does addressing them cease being a fancy and begin to make sense.

But responsibility toward the dead extends further than just addressing them in our formulae of contrition. There is a more definite sense in which we must express fidelity toward the men and women, the "saints," who have gone before us, and whom we recognize as exemplars of the way we ourselves should live. I would attempt to capture this responsibility, this fidelity, in the following words: Insofar as they have shown us how to live, when we profess to live a Christian life, *we owe these men and women, these saints, a debt.* It is here, I think, with this idea, that we can also begin to fulfill the promise made above to discuss in a more subjective and immediately affective fashion just what our personal involvement with the dead might include. In other words, while we have just finished listing some points that the idea of petitioning the dead presumes about their *present* existence (their life in heaven), we are now ready to discuss their *past* existence (their life on earth) and how it might influence us.

The saints are the witnesses of our faith. They demonstrate to us the good we should do, and the wrong we should avoid, in attempting to live like Christ. They indicate the magnanimity, the humility, the generosity—in a word, the lack of self-concern—this Christlikeness entails. Yet they also indicate that this Christlikeness is not procured easily; that it demands fidelity and attention, effort and sacrifice. No one who has read the words of a "canonized" Paul or Thomas or Teresa, or the words of an "uncanonized" Pascal or Luther or Kierkegaard would care to deny this. On their every page lies the truth that being like Christ is arduous; that an army of contrary inclinations lies in wait to impede one's progress. The tale of a saint is never a pretty one, pretentious or self-satisfied. It tells of fears and frustrations, of doubts and disappointments, of constant labor to be like the Lord.

It is a mistake, therefore, to attempt to "dehumanize" the saints, as so often happens in recounting their lives. It is misguided to think they were born to Christian living; that they were not the constant prey of self-concern; that their pursuit of Christlikeness was any the easier than ours. Such thinking does them a terrible injustice, because saints are individuals born like all others. What makes them different, what makes them saints, is not what they are born but what they become, what they do with their lives: what values they work to create and sustain, what vices they work to overcome. It is the good within them that they encourage, and the wrong for which they are contrite, that sets saintly individuals apart from others. It is in the regret they feel for their wickedness, and their committed striving to amend it, that they become for us exemplars of Christian life.

To acknowledge the saints in our confession of contrition is thus quite appropriate. It is to admit that we have been unfaithful to the example they have provided us. It is to say: "Your whole life witnesses to the fact that being like Christ is a struggle, but a struggle worth the effort. For this witness you have set before us, and for our infidelity to it, we are contrite. And our contrition will not be mere empty words, but an effort to amend our lives according to the witness you have given." It is to a memory that we are here confessing, to be sure; but it is a memory that is alive, a presence actively affecting how we think, feel and act. It is a memory complementing the conscious, personal existence which in faith we assert the dead now enjoy.

Before the saints, therefore, this one stance is proper above all: the humility born of being a good student. When we pray to the saints we should pray first to learn from them; to recognize their experience and appreciate their wisdom; to take seriously the Christlikeness they enfleshed. When we think of the saints we should think first of what they offer us, how we might make their witness our own.

We do not demand, however, that the saints respond to these prayers and thoughts, this confession. For no response is needed; the confession itself is sufficient. The awareness it indicates of the responsibility we owe to those who have gone before us, and of the way we have failed this responsibility, is what makes our confession an act of contrition, a statement of regret and amendment. For by it we are recognizing that we do indeed owe the dead regret for our infidelity to their witness to Christ; that we do indeed owe them the amendment of our lives that says their witness has not gone for naught. Indeed, both of these together, our regret and amendment, our contrition before the saints, compose the finest expression of fidelity we can pay them. It is to say that we not only acknowledge their existence, but that their existence matters to us *now,* influencing the way we presently think and behave. Aside from martyrdom in their name, what greater honor than this can be given to the dead, to say, "You live on in me"?

For these reasons I think it is then unfortunate that in recent years popular piety with reference to the saints has become so barren. The devotions that marked our past are now seldom present, and nothing, no new "form" has as yet taken their place. It is true, of course, that in the past these devotions—the so-called "cult of the Virgin" and "cult of the saints"—were sometimes ill-conceived and produced abuses in practice. There was frequently a too-intense identification with the saints, a blind imitation of the details of their behavior, an uncritical acceptance of the specifics of their thought- and feeling-patterns. This in turn often led to a nostalgia in which people lost touch with their own concrete situation, the needs and demands of present time and place. As an expression of humility, for example, individuals would crawl on their knees up the stairs of a church, when taming their ambitions or slandering tongues would have been much more appropriate. Furthermore, there is always something seriously amiss whenever the centricity of Christ in a Christian spirituality is displaced by the Virgin or one of the saints. The result is disorientation, a loss of the matrix around which Christian life, in all its dimensions, must necessarily revolve if it is to maintain its identity.

Nevertheless, in maintaining this centricity of Christ we should still not diminish into unimportance the witness that the saints also offer us for Christian living. This would be to go to an extreme exactly opposite that above, when what is called for is balance. While Christ must unquestionably possess priority in our spiritual life, the saints too should possess a place, one of honor, not insignificance. For they provide us with a concrete expression of what a person might be like when he or she has in fact made Christ the central consideration in life. The saint is a *locus Christi,* a place in which Christ is to some extent manifested. From him or her, therefore, we can always learn something of what it means to be a Christian in a world that forever changes: something of generosity and humility, of faith, hope and love; something of contrition, of regret for sin and the ways sin can be amended. The saint is an exemplar, a specific instance of the meaning of Christlikeness. As Christ himself in some fashion enfleshes God in a particular life, so the saint in some fashion enfleshes Christ in a particular life—as when St. Paul says, for example, "It is no longer I who live but Christ who lives in me" (Gal 2:20).

The Need for Guidance

It is this dependence on the saint, therefore, this looking toward him for guidance in Christian living, that I would suggest as the foremost meaning of the idea of petitioning the dead. To ask something of someone is an expression of our dependence on him; specifically, we are depending on him to fulfill the request being made. But from this specific instance of our dependence—that is, regarding the particular request we seek—I think we can extend the idea of our dependence to include a broader compass. Our request then comes to be seen as only one instance of that whole phenomenon which is our need for others, our dependence on them for guidance and aid.

For we are not born with a knowledge of how to live. We must discover it elsewhere, not within ourselves. If we wish to know how to live like an eastern sage, we go to the East, to seek out the wisdom and teachings of a Buddha, a Lao-tzu, a Confucius, and their followers. If we wish to know how to live like a Marxist, we go to the books and teachings of Marx and the witness of his followers, a Lenin or Mao or Marcuse. So too, if we wish to learn how to live like a Christian, we go to Christ; we seek out the scriptures and the witness which his followers, the saints, provide. We are not born a sage or a Marxist—or a Christian. We are born only breathing, whimpering flesh. To become what we desire, we must learn from others; we must discover it in them.

We have argued throughout this book that if in contrition we are essentially asking forgiveness of sins, then we must address this contrition to all against whom we have sinned. Thus, I confess my contrition to God, or to the particular persons whom I have wronged. Now we must ask whether these persons include the saints, the dead who have gone before us. Can we sin against these men and women? If, as we have maintained, we can only sin against persons within particular contexts that arise in our lives—that is, against persons who interact with us in present situations—can the saints be understood as fulfilling this condition? The question as phrased defies a definite answer, since any answer would depend on the degree of the relationship, the extent to which it is personally conceived, between the individual and the saint now living "in heaven." If the relationship is intimate, the individual might well feel he has sinned against a Francis or Teresa, for example, by a promise broken or a vow unfulfilled. On the other hand, an individual would hardly feel he has sinned against these or any of the saints if their very names were only vaguely, if at all, familiar to him.

But if contrition likewise involves the commitment to amend one's life, as we have also maintained, it would indeed seem appropriate to include the saints in our contrition. We would include them to the extent that our amendment must always include a searching for guidance in Christian living, in what it means to be faithful to the person and message of Jesus. For it is nothing less than Christlikeness which he is first seeking whenever a Christian confesses contrition. We regret the sin that has shown us distant from Christ; we desire the amendment that will lessen this distance. But this regret that we experience, this amendment that we desire—to understand these we must first become docile, students willing to learn, first from Christ himself, and then from those who have followed Christ, unto death and holiness. We must become, in short, faithful heirs to those who have gone before us.

2. Petitioning the Living

Our reflections in this section will return us to a group of individuals with whom we were also concerned in chapter one, namely, our "brothers and sisters." There we were concerned with confessing contrition to them; here we will be concerned with making a request of them. Yet the two concerns, we will suggest, are largely interrelated. It is because I have sinned against others that I now find myself in a position of supplication before them. Again, however, what this fully means will not become clear until we reach the next section, where we will more thoroughly examine what it is we are requesting. But as with the idea of petitioning the dead, I think the idea of petitioning the living also merits consideration on its own.

In what kind of relationship does this petitioning place us with regard to our brothers and sisters? Certainly one similar to that mentioned in the last section, when discussing our relationship to the saints, the dead who have gone before us: namely, a relationship of dependence. In the request we make of them, in what we seek, we are affirming that we are not sufficient unto ourselves, but need help and assistance. We are contradicting, in other words, that inclination toward an excessive sense of autonomy that we discussed in the last chapter. For if the excessively autonomous self is marked by an unqualified assertion of its self-reliance, of being an island unto itself, independent and without need of others, the self that must ask aid of others presents us with a much different picture. The asking self, the begging, pleading, or praying self knows that it cannot afford the luxury of excessive self-reliance; that it is not radically autonomous or independent; that it requires others to become what it desires to be.

A Common Center, a Common Striving

The help that we ask of the living is first and above all the same that we ask of the saints. It is the help of their witness to Christian living. We turn to them seeking that expression of Christlikeness which we desire to demonstrate in our own lives. They may not be "canonical" saints, universally recognized for their Christian living. But they are saints in the sense that we are dependent on them for the witness they give—a witness we have judged worthy of study and emulation. It is these living saints, therefore, rather than the indifferent and unconcerned within the Christian community, that we are addressing whenever we request the prayer, the help and assistance, of our "brothers and sisters."

A person need not be dead before we can perceive saintliness in him; in fact, death removes the saint a step away from us. We can no longer see or hear or touch him. We can no longer watch his response to various issues, no longer observe his values expressed in changing situations. His death has made of his life a finished cycle, a closed book. Now we can only imagine how he might respond to present issues and situations; now we can only construe these responses on the basis of his past actions.

We have, I think, a generally accepted example of a living saint in the awesome figure of Mother Teresa of Calcutta. In her work with the poor and underprivileged, in her self-sacrifice and care for them as her children, she has struck a responsive chord in the hearts of all who are seeking what it means to live a Christian life. She has made of her life, as a title of a recent book indicates, something beautiful for God. She herself may not care for the attention she gets. But that is not the point; it is likely but another expression of the spirit of selflessness which guides her life. What is important about her is that others depend on her for an example of Christlikeness as she performs her mission. Christ said to feed the hungry, and she is willing. Christ said to clothe the naked, shelter the homeless, care for the sick and dying, and she obeys. Christ said to seek not the praise of men, show yourself meek, your heart humble, and she assents.

Mother Teresa is only one example among many I could have chosen; and only one of many more, had others also been choosing. She is perhaps the most publicized example—thanks in large part to a *Time* cover story of two or three years ago. But I for one also know a man down the street who in his own life is witnessing as much as she to Christlikeness. And he has greater influence on me precisely because his witness is far more accessible than hers; it is directly available to me on a day-to-day basis. I can actually see and hear him, and study in close detail that frame of mind, that attitude of self-giving, generosity and humility which I call Christlikeness. To me, like Mother Teresa, this man is as much a saint as a Paul or Francis or Peter Damien. I am dependent upon him for his witness, for learning the ways of Christ in today's world. Like the Samaritan in the parable of Jesus, from whom the injured man learns the meaning of charity, I am learning the meaning of love from this man. Like the Samaritan with whom the injured man came into direct contact—whose kindness the injured man did not need to read of in books or hear told of by others—I experience directly the kindness of this man. I myself can and do concretely relate to him. No mediation is required; he is not a step removed from me by death or distance.

What I ask of him, however, I do not ask directly. I ask it in secret, in my own mind. I ask that I be allowed to continue learning from this man; that his witness not be removed from my direct observation; that I may continue to study and relate to him. But I do not confess this request to him personally, since it would serve no purpose, save to place him at one pole of a relationship that would likely embarrass and disconcert him. His humility would rebel against the thought that he was the teacher of my spirit. And while I was thinking of the virtue I found in him, he would be thinking of his vice; while I was seeing his selflessness, he would be seeing his self-concern; while I stood docile before his sanctity, he would stand shamed before his sin. My request, therefore, is a desire, a need, a prayer that I voice to myself, or to another with whom I enjoy utter confidence. For in contrition, in seeking the aid of others to amend my life, I am never in the business of embarrassing or disconcerting them—that is not a basis upon which any relationship can succeed.

One further point—a critical one—must also be noted about petitioning aid in contrition from the living. It is indicated by the very use of the word "living"—which we have been reducing more specifically to the words, "my brothers and sisters." The words are plural; they connote a gathering together, a grouping; in short, a community. Consequently, my request is being made not just of this or that particular individual, but of all the members of the community to which I am confessing. Furthermore, the words indicate that I possess a certain sense of solidarity with these men and women that allows me to make my request, to call upon their aid and assistance. There is a sense of union with them that does not make of my request an affront, or worse, a meaningless presumption. It is the same sense of solidarity and union that we described in chapter one: the solidarity and union that are derived from any common faith in God; the confession that God gave and sustains our lives, and in Christ has offered us a way to save ourselves.

Now I may, of course, isolate from this community particular individuals insofar as they meet the specifics of my request. This is what I myself have done, of course, in the case of the man above. But in the general expression of my need, my dependence upon others in assisting and guiding me in my Christian life, I address my request to the entire community. I am saying in effect: "I ask all of you to help me in whatever way each of you and all of you together can. I cannot stand alone in pursuing Christlikeness; I can only stand among you, amidst the support you can give me. In my trying to be like Christ I am not self-sufficient but reliant; I must secure help from wherever I might receive it, from whoever is willing to give it. Above all, this is the case in my contrition for sin. For often I am not even aware of the sin I have committed, and so can feel no sorrow for it, let alone a need to amend it. I need a catalyst, therefore, an outside influence, someone who will show me where I have been remiss and how I should rectify it."

This community of individuals upon which each of us relies is what we might otherwise call the "church." The church is the gathering of men and women, "brothers and sisters," whose common center is the person of Christ, and whose common striving is for Christlikeness. How each specifically conceives this center and engages this striving may vary widely. But the center and the striving are held in common, and certain fundamental assertions can be made about each. These assertions, in fact, are a prerequisite. For without them our common center and striving would remain vacuous, void of meaning. The skeleton would have no flesh. There would be no definite, solid referents to which we could point and say: This we all share, and in sharing them we are a community. Except in misguided imagination, however, or playful fancy, the church could clearly not exist if this were the situation.

Thus we would all share, for example, the idea that striving for Christlikeness involves attitudes of generosity and humility, a lack of self-concern. And we would all share the idea that Christ himself is the paradigm of these attitudes, enacting them without failure, and so in some way completely unlike us. We would all share, too, the idea that for a further understanding of what this common center and striving mean, each member of the church is dependent on others: to instruct and inform him; to encourage and sustain him; to demonstrate the many ways in which the center and striving affect and characterize his existence.

The above are just three of the more obvious referents that bind Christians into a community. While recognizing that petulance which is forever ready to qualify or dispute anything, to my mind they are inarguable. Other referents, of course, are not nearly so obvious; and legitimate debate over them has often led to subgroupings within the Christian community. I am thinking, for example, of disputes that have arisen over the specific meaning of doctrines such as the Trinity, grace, atonement, and so on. But these, I think, while often involving important issues and consequences, should be seen as secondary to the shared and common referents that all Christians confess. The critical, often subliminal affirmations that make us one, a church, should always merit conscious and constant priority in our thoughts and actions.

Interlude: Naming the Lord Jesus

In light of the above comments, and indeed of our reflections throughout this book, it would now seem appropriate to raise and confront a peculiar but obvious historical fact about many of our common formulae for contrition. It is this, bluntly put: Nowhere do these formulae cite the name of Jesus. They are addressed to God, to Mary, the angels, the saints, our "brothers and sisters." But nowhere is the person of Christ mentioned.* At least initially, this might prove a disturbing omission. Anyone, I imagine, might fairly expect that in a common Christian formula of contrition, in a prayer that might otherwise be profoundly God- and church-oriented, the name of Jesus would occupy a focal if not repeated place. If Christ is in fact the common center of our lives, and Christlikeness the goal of our common striving, then in something so important as a formula for contrition his name should be noted not by its absence but by its presence.

---

* I am thinking, for example, of the formula cited at the beginning of this chapter, as well as the more traditional one that begins, "O my God, I am heartily sorry for having offended Thee. . . ."

Of course, despite this absence of his name in various formulae, we still recognize that the person, the influence of Christ must clearly pervade any expression of Christian contrition. This has been our repeated bias throughout this book, insofar as we have consistently judged what constitutes our fault and sin by the words and deeds, the witness of Christ. In doing so we have been especially concerned with isolating his generosity and humility, and with suggesting that each of these may in turn be approached as but one expression of that even more singular quality of his: namely, his lack of self-concern. If only in this key area of our reflections—in determining a rubric for understanding fault and sin—Christ has transparently occupied a central position. He provides the milieu, the environment within which the Christian decides whether he has acted well or badly, with virtue or vice. He provides the pattern outlining the amendment that must take place whenever the Christian is contrite for his sin.

I can imagine the omission of the name of Jesus, therefore, only because his presence must so effectively dominate any Christian formula of contrition that to specify him by name is judged unnecessary or redundant. But this is an adequate explanation only when we do not focus all our attention on the words themselves of the formula. It requires, that is, a placing of the words in a Christ-centered consciousness, so that as each of the phrases of the formula passes through our minds we interpret it through the medium of this consciousness. This is what I meant above when I spoke of Christ as the milieu of any Christian formula of contrition, and the basis on which our sorrow for sins, and especially our amendment of them, must be found. Because this milieu, this basis might go unnamed, then, it is not for that reason any the less present, any the less influential. I am reminded of the words spoken by the Ancient of Days in the Book of Revelation: "I am the Alpha and the Omega, the Beginning and the End." So it is with Christ; he circumscribes the whole of our contrition, a presence to it from beginning to end.

For surely as Christians we must first and last confess our sin to Christ, from whom we draw our name. Surely as Christians we must first and last seek guidance from Christ, from whom we draw our name. And surely as Christians we must first and last be grateful for Christ, from whom we draw our name. Unless our name, Christian, means little or nothing to us; unless it is a word to which we attach little or no significance; unless we are indifferent to what we are called and call ourselves: Jesus must be a living and effective presence in all we are and desire to become.

And so must he plainly be in our contrition. Because contrition is nothing if not a formative process, a shaping of our selves. Through regret for the wrong we have committed, and through the desire to amend it, we are engaged in the task of changing what we now are for the sake of what we want to be. At the center of this process, this task of self-formation, resides the person, the presence of Christ, guiding and strengthening. Otherwise let us not call ourselves Christians, and our common striving a striving for Christlikeness.

It is sometimes easy, of course, to lose sight of Christ in our immediate concerns, our day-to-day relationships with our "brothers and sisters," that community we have called the church. Nonetheless, the saving thought must still remain and keep constantly emerging: The whole, the whole of the community, cannot hold together unless it remains consciously centered. Should it lose sight of this center, should it cease being consciously oriented toward its source, the community which is Christ's church must inevitably disappear, or become something else, someone else's church, or perhaps a good-will organization. To maintain its identity, to make sense of its calling itself

"Christian," the church must first be consciously faithful to him from whom it derives. Its primary and overriding task must be to sustain as a living presence among its members the person, words and deeds of Jesus. And its primary and overriding goal must ever be to encourage its members toward a greater, more inclusive appropriation of Christ-likeness in their lives.

The Anonymous Christian

It is the apparent plainness of the above point that makes me so wary of all ideas of "anonymous Christianity" or "the anonymous Christian." It is true, of course, that we may construct a theology of grace in which the person of Christ plays the pivotal role (Christ is the "mediator" of grace). It is also true that we may then say that whoever receives this grace *by the mere fact of its reception* is thereby "Christianized." Furthermore, although such a theology is exactly what we said it was, a construct, it at least has the merit of offering an explanation of grace that yet retains an essential place for Christ. As such we can have no argument with it; our wariness is not yet born. If we understand grace as basically *what* allows us to be saved, and if we understand Christ as the exemplar in word and deed of *how* we can be saved, then the bond between grace and Christ is established. Christ is rightly called a mediator, a demonstrator, of what allows us to be saved.

Our wariness over the construct, then, is not with the question *through* whom this grace is bestowed; it is bestowed through Christ. Rather, our wariness begins to surface with the question *upon* whom it is bestowed. More specifically, it involves the idea that the receptor of this grace may be completely passive in the face of its reception. By this I mean that while *we* may assert what has happened to him through Christ—he has been favored by God—*he*

himself may not or need not assert it. Without ever having
to be conscious of it, in other words, he has been "Christianized" by the grace, the favor of God. To be sure, he
may be conscious of the grace itself, the favor. He may be
aware that somehow he has been blessed. Something in his
mind or heart "clicks," a thought, a feeling, and he knows
that God has touched his life and shown him the way to be
saved. But in no way does he connect this with the person
of Christ; his thoughts, his feelings, his consciousness are
completely a-Christic. Yet despite this, so our construct
says, despite his own unawareness, this individual is still a
Christian, an "anonymous Christian," a Christian who does
not consciously center his life on Christ.

Now our wariness is full born, and we must finally
demur. Our argument is not with the freedom with which
God graces men and women. It is definitely not with the
idea that all *can* be graced: For who would dare decide the
possibilities of God? No, our argument is with the abuse
of the word "Christian." To my mind the word can only
be applied to an individual whose life is centered on Christ,
whose striving is for Christlikeness in how he thinks, feels
and acts. But this clearly calls for a conscious centeredness.
By grace alone, in other words, an individual does not become Christ-oriented automatically, without effort, willy-
nilly. Rather, he must be faithful to the grace, and the
possibility it provides for Christlikeness, *in a conscientious
way*. To be a Christian is to respond to the favor of God,
and the possibilities it offers us, in a manner that intentionally appropriates the witness, the words and deeds, set us by
Christ. Otherwise, and without hesitation, one might still
be called a graced being, as Abraham, for example, Moses
and Gandhi were presumably graced beings. But unless
the phrase "anonymous Christian" somehow ceases being a
contradiction in terms, which I don't think it can, one could
hardly be called a Christian.

A Christian confession of contrition makes no sense unless it is centered on Christ. In contrition we can appreciate the place of God, the saints, our "brothers and sisters" only because Christ, by word and deed, has shown us something of its essential meaning. His demonstration, of course, is not always as lucid as we might like; it is often blurred and uncertain to us, living now in the 20th century. But enough of it is certain to provide a basis for understanding what it means to be Christlike. How could anyone fail to see, for example, that it involves generosity and humility, a lack of self-concern?

When as Christians we confess regret for our sins and the desire to amend our lives, we do so with Christ at the center of our consciousness. We confess our contrition not without reason, then, and not for any reason, but for this reason, and this above all: because we desire to be Christlike. And it is the favor of God, the grace, the possibility held out to us that we can be Christlike, that impels us to this confession.

3. Petitioning Prayer

With this idea of petitioning prayer our reflections in this chapter will be complete. It states the specific request we make of the living and the dead, and establishes our dependence on others insofar as they are able to mediate our relationship to God. What we are acknowledging by our request is that before God we cannot stand alone but are in need of help, the care and interest, the prayers of others. What we are asking, therefore, is that these others become directly involved in the formation of our spirit; that they take part in what we become; that they offer us strength and consolation, desire and a spirit of contrition, whenever we acknowledge the virtue and vice within us.

Before God, and because of this involvement with us, we ask that they witness to our sincerity in becoming more Christlike.

The Intercession of Others

By way of further explanation, I would now like to offer a concrete example of the above idea, our need for the intercessory help of others. It requires throughout that we bear in mind that the phenomenon we have been studying is confession of contrition for sin, an acknowledgment of wrongdoing that includes both regret and a promise of amendment.

Let us say there is a teenage boy, one close to manhood, who has deliberately and quite seriously misbehaved. Let us also say, however, that after a while he begins to feel regret for the way he has acted—for the disappointment and anger and frustration he has caused his parents. He now realizes that he has acted wrongly, without excuse or justification, with no one to blame but himself. And he now wishes to make amends for this misbehavior, to express his regret in word and deed. He rightly senses, and is disturbed by, the estrangement that has been created between him and his parents. He sincerely wants to overcome it; but because of the present feelings of his parents, which he construes as the barrier, he is reluctant to make a direct approach. Yet he also knows that the initiative, however indirect, is his responsibility. So what does he do? He enlists the services of his sister, who is only slightly older than himself. He asks her to go to their parents, and to express his contrition for him. He knows that at the time no barrier of hurt feelings exists between her and their parents, that she has a direct access to them and can speak freely to them. She will become the one upon whom he depends for the initiative he seeks, his mediator, his liaison for expressing his contrition. She will become his first voice in confessing that he has acted wrongly, in affirming his sorrow, and in expressing the promised amendment of his behavior. And because his parents and his relationship with them are presently uppermost in his mind, no pride or bitter memories will stand in the way of his asking her to help, to intercede for him. All their own previous conflicts will be set aside, at least in his own mind, for the sake of the assistance he now needs. It is, after all, a question of priorities; and he is not so wicked as to put his pride or past hurts before a renewed intimacy with his parents.

But there is still another consideration. He has reflected that if his sister acts as his mediator, his contrition will more likely be accepted by his parents than if he immediately voiced it himself. For he knows that he will first have to confess it to her before she can go to their parents. And he knows her well enough: If she is not convinced by the sincerity of his regret and desire to amend, she will not fulfill his request. She will not lie for him; she will not even bias her account in his favor. But he also knows—and here is where his hope resides—that his parents, too, are aware of this. If she comes before them expressing his contrition they will accept by this very fact that he is sincere.

In his sister, then, the young man has found a perfect ally for initiating the contrition he wishes to demonstrate to his parents. Through her he can take the first step in expressing his regret for the wrong he has done and his intention to amend it. Afterwards he can then approach them personally and confess for himself, in word and deed, the contrition he has experienced.

Something similar to the above situation can guide our interpretation of the idea of seeking aid in our contrition before God. We ask others to pray for us to God in order to demonstrate the sincerity of our contrition. It is not enough, we think, merely to say words of contrition. We must be able to "back them up"; to demonstrate that we mean what we say. When we express our contrition to others, and then have them pray to God for us, their prayer provides this demonstration, at least initially. It indicates that we have willingly taken the first step of contrition: namely, an acceptance of the fact that to amend the sin we regret we must depend upon the help of others. Unlike our example of the young man and his parents, however, we take this step not for the sake of God—God does not isolate himself from us because of our sin, and he is certainly not hurt or harmed by it—but for our own sake. We take it, that is, because we know it is the first requirement testing all sincere contrition. Whenever we fail to acknowledge at the very beginning of our contrition that we need help in amending the sin we regret, we have fallen prey to the seduction of autonomy, to thinking that we are sufficient unto ourselves. At this point, if our reflections in the previous two sections were at all valid, we have only one option open to us: We must stop and begin our contrition anew.

But more can be drawn from our example. If the young man's sister really cares for him, if she is distressed by the estrangement that occurs between her parents and her brother when he misbehaves, she will take a personal part in the contrition he desires to express. She will actively seek to help him in fulfilling it, by taking it as seriously as he. Furthermore, she too will forget her own bitter memories of their past relationship. In their place she will exercise sympathy and understanding toward him, a willingness to help, a loyalty to his regret and promise to amend. She knows, of course, that she cannot be too direct in this, let alone harsh and demanding. Not only would he resent this approach, but it would have too much the flavor of hypocrisy. For she readily admits, at least to herself, that her own relationship with her parents has itself been often marked by failure and wrongdoing. No, her approach must be indirect, her guidance gentle. It must be that of setting a good example in what she herself says and does: no more the uncivil tongue, no more the selfish disobedience, no more the arrogance of always being in the right. A kind-thinking generosity and humility: These are the guides of her own behavior that she will set before him, the brother she loves.

It is the attitude of this sister that I think must also prevail in the community which is the Christian church. Toward the individual confessing contrition for sin the members of this community must willingly offer their assistance. This is nothing less than an integral part both of their conviction that the person is indeed contrite, and of their responsibility toward that person as one of their "brothers and sisters." To go before God and pray *for* the sinner, therefore, is to be accountable *with* the sinner. It is to say to God something like: "We are convinced of his sincerity in contrition, his regret for his sin and desire to amend it. And on his part we ask that your grace, your favor, be made accessible to him; that he have the strength to nourish his virtue and overcome his vice; that his striving for Christ-likeness be blessed." In his prayer each member of the community freely involves himself in the contrition that any other member confesses.

But the greatest responsibility, of course, always remains with the one confessing: This has been our constant theme. It is he, after all, who must be the agent of his own amendment; no one can do it for him, just as no one can feel his regret for him. The task to amend is his because the desire is his. He cannot slough it off. He cannot place himself in the hands of others, with the idea that should he continue in his sin the blame is theirs. For even though others may claim some responsibility for the wrong he commits, he himself cannot claim it for them. He cannot in this sense share his contrition. He cannot "lose" it among the members of the community, thinking that their prayers, their commitment to help, absolves him from his own regret and need to amend. But, knowing his need, he will say without hesitation: "I ask you, my brothers and sisters, to pray for me to the Lord our God: to aid my fidelity to the grace made accessible to me; to aid my strength in nourishing virtue and overcoming vice; to aid in all things my striving for Christlikeness." No pride will prevent this request, no arrogance stand in its way. In asking for the prayers, the help of his brothers and sisters, the individual has forsworn the option for self-sufficiency, the idea that he can "go it alone." His request indicates that he can only go where he desires, to Christlikeness, with others.

Tropistic Prayer

It is now clear, I imagine, that the idea of prayer is much more extensive than we might initially think. Ordinarily we understand prayer to be a set of words, a prescribed or spontaneous recitation that is addressed to God or Jesus or the saints at particular times and in particular situations. With this understanding we have no argument. Prayer indeed involves specific times and contexts: thoughts voiced or unvoiced, for example, in a church, or by a death bed, or before an important event. It is a specific verbal response that we judge appropriate to such moments and contexts: that God is kind and provident, or that this child not die, or that I succeed at the task I am now beginning. Yet still a question remains, and we cannot end by shirking it. For while we admit that this understanding of prayer is a correct one, can we admit that it is a sufficient one? Is this all there is to prayer? Does it satisfy us?

If we are to remain faithful to our reflections so far, we must respond negatively to these questions. Prayer is not merely a matter of words employed at certain moments and in certain situations; it is far more inclusive of the rest of our lives. These specific acts, therefore, might more properly be called "prayers," while prayer as such would be the state of mind of which these acts are but particular forms. Prayer, in other words, describes an *attitude;* it is a pattern of thinking, feeling and doing that encompasses our whole existence, not just a part of it. It is a way of life; something that shapes us more than something we shape. It enters into the very definition of ourselves; more than something we do, it is a component part of what we are.

What is this pattern or attitude or state of mind that describes prayer? I would describe it by the single word "willingness," a willingness characterized by responsiveness, or by a word I also like, "tropism."

Let us look at this word "tropism" a bit more closely. According to *Webster's* dictionary, the first definition of tropism reads: "an involuntary movement of an organism or any of its parts involving turning or curvature and induced either automatically or in response to stimuli, as a chemical agent, light, etc." We say, for example, that certain plants are *heliotropic,* meaning that their leaves always bend toward a given source of light. Slowly or quickly, depending upon the strength of the source, this movement is inexorable. It will always happen; it will be stilled only by the organism's death. Anyone who has been frustrated over the arrangement of house plants knows clearly enough what I mean. During spring and summer their leaves favor a northern exposure; during autumn and winter a southern. Turning, always turning as the seasons pass, the leaves will adjust to the source of light, no matter how fervid the attempt to keep them confined to a single pattern.

This first definition gives us something of the meaning I have in mind when I say that prayer as willingness is tropistic. The second definition clarifies this meaning even further. Tropism is "any innate tendency to react in a definite manner to stimuli." This definition is more general than the first, and so less oriented toward the specific mechanics of chemistry and biology. As such it may be more readily applied to human attitudes.

The key word, of course, is "innate." This is a qualitative adjective initially meant to describe any trait or distinct characteristic that an individual apparently possesses from birth and habitually expresses. We speak, for example, of the innate protectiveness that emerges when a human female has a child; or of the innate intelligence of the child who masters every project receiving his attention; or of the innate talent of the man who plays, but has never studied, the violin. But the word can also describe a trait or characteristic that the individual has acquired, and only afterwards habitually expresses. Here we speak, for example, of a person's innate humor or vindictiveness, his optimism or pessimism. The first type of innate characteristic is possessed without effort; the second demands discipline, a process of failure and success.

When I say that prayer is tropistic, then, I mean that it is defined by an innate willingness to respond in a certain fashion to our surrounding world, the events and people that shape our lives. Clearly, however, I am defining it as innate in the second sense above. No one is born with this willingness, as he might be with musical talent. No, prayer is not dependent on the mere fact of birth, but on effort. It is an acquired characteristic, not a natural one, a spirit of responsiveness that takes time, a long time, to nourish before it becomes habitual. But I must also emphasize that this spirit involves not just any type of response, but a certain type. In prayer the individual's response to the people and events that shape life is neither blind nor variously motivated. It has a basis, a particular motive that guides it.

What might this response be? The answer is now easily offered. It is the response to which we have repeatedly referred throughout this book: the response of generosity and humility, a lack of self-concern. Prayer understood as willing responsiveness is the habitual turning toward others and toward God in service to them. It is the willing humility that places concern for others before self-concern; the responsive generosity that gives of our time and talents to the care and well-being of others.

It is from this state of mind, these attitudes of generosity and humility, that many of our particular "prayers" will then emerge. They express in a specific fashion, in certain moments and situations, the humility we practice before God and other persons. They ask forgiveness of sin, for example, or assistance in virtue; they indicate our willingness to be dependent on others, our recognition that we cannot stand alone. They express as well the generosity we practice before God and other persons. They place us at the service of God's will, for example, or indicate our responsiveness to those in need. Just as our "prayers" of humility, in other words, verbalize our willingness to be dependent on others, so our "prayers" of generosity verbalize our willingness to let others be dependent on us. Each in its own way demonstrates that lack of self-concern which is the foremost mark of Christlikeness.

In the understanding I would offer, then, prayer is nothing less than a pattern of life; if you will, a life-style. It is not confined to times and seasons, places and particular contexts. It is pervasive. It imbues the whole of the individual's existence as a continuing state of mind—the state of mind St. Paul encourages when he teaches us to "pray always" (1 Thes 5:17). It is the attitude we intend to capture when we say of someone that his life is a "life of prayer." We do not say that his life is a life which includes prayer; or that his life is a life in which prayer has a place.

We say that his life itself is prayer. In saying this we clearly intend to indicate that prayer is first defined by its constancy; by its being a set attitude that is only subsequently expressed in a ritual or spontaneous formula or deed. Any given formula of contrition, then, will be only one expression of a basic state of mind that it presumes is already present in the individual. It is only one of a whole host of "prayers" we might use to indicate our regret for sin and the desire to amend it. The point is, none of these formulae will serve any purpose, all will be empty, mere formulae, if they are not undergirded by something like that attitude of prayer discussed above: an innate responsiveness, marked by generosity and humility, to the people and events that shape our lives.

When in contrition, therefore, we ask our brothers and sisters to pray for us, we do not mean that they take time out and address some words to God on our behalf. Or more correctly, we do not mean that they do only that. What we are asking of them is something much more. We are asking that they take an attitude toward us of humility and generosity, a lack of self-concern. Even more, we are asking that this attitude be not terminal but constant—because we are not just now and then dependent on it; we are always dependent on it.

Union in Contrition

In conclusion, let us recall how in chapter one we suggested that the idea of our being brothers and sisters to each other was based on the acceptance of our common source in God. We still affirm this basis, of course—but only as far as it goes. For unless the above comments remain unapplied, we must now broaden it. We must now say that our being brothers and sisters to each other is based not only on our common source in God, but also on our lifelong relationship of dependence on one another—specifically, our dependence on one another's willing humility and generosity.

But if we ask of our brothers and sisters that their prayer be a life of humility and generosity toward us, then they in turn are asking the very same thing of us when they voice their own need. Just as our request places a responsibility on them, so their request places a responsibility on us. Thus we become involved in a relationship defined by its reciprocity, its mutuality. No one, in other words, stands alone in his contrition. All stand together, united by the need of each for the willing selflessness of his brothers and sisters. For without this willingness regret remains sterile. Receiving no reception, no strength from the community, it cannot issue in that full-born amendment of sin that it desires.

It is this interdependence, this willingness to be humble and generous toward one another, this responsiveness to one another marked by a lack of self-concern, that describes the community, the church, that is centered on Christ and strives continually to be Christlike. Alone we must take responsibility for our sin; that is certain. Our sin is our own. But to regret and amend our sin, to become more and more like the Lord we worship—for this we need one another.

Final Words:
Our Responsibility and Community

A woman came to me one day for confessional counseling. She had been to see me several times previously, and in the course of these meetings had recited a near litany of the wrongs she had committed over the course of many years. At first I was perplexed by her recitals and the details she saw fit to include. It was as if she had kept a day-to-day diary of her sins. But after a while I went from being perplexed to being disturbed. For I became aware that despite her honesty, her studied intention to mention all she could remember, her monologues indicated not a trace of contrition, no regret, no desire to change her ways. She was simply giving me the facts, like an accountant tallying up debits in a business meeting.

When I finally confronted her with this impression, her response was quick and to the point. She said that reciting her wrongdoing, "clearing the slate" of her sins, was for her a sufficient enough definition of contrition. What was done, was done. There was no use in crying over spilled milk, and certainly no sense it letting it affect the future. If I was going to start "badgering" her (as she put it) about not feeling any sorrow, or about being a better person in the future, she would then and there end meeting with me. Nowhere could I detect the slightest remorse for what she had done; nowhere the slightest intent to improve how she thought, felt and acted. On the contrary, I had every reason to believe that she would go on living precisely as she always had.

I don't know how often experiences like mine with this woman have occurred to other ministers or counselors. But they have happened often enough to me to form the basis for my once writing a rather somber, somewhat cynical poem. I entitled it "Absolution," and it reads as follows:

Purple stole now drapes my neck—
I absolve you from your sins,
the same that I commit
though I am Christ the sinless.

And for your penance
try to do better.
Nothing too strict
for fear of my own soul.

A manufacturer's method
in and out
the finished product
a whitened soul bleached by my words
and the wave of a hand

Dismissal
and life is lived as before.*

---

* This poem first appeared in *The Christian Century,* vol. XCIII, no. 5 (February 18, 1976), p. 146, and is reprinted here by permission.

Experiences like these, I must admit, also underlie my writing of this book. In it I have set out to show that contrition is not a mere recitation of wrongdoing, but an exercise, a "spiritual exercise," involving subjective engagement. To be contrite is not the same as to be tall or short or thin. It is not a description of oneself "out there," an objective fact about oneself that demands little if any committed involvement.

If I have had one overwhelming purpose in the foregoing chapters, then, it has been to encourage this involvement. My reflections throughout have been personal rather than scholarly in tone and orientation. This was deliberate, so as to provide a catalyst toward further reflection by as many readers as possible. Whether or not the reader agrees with all I have said, therefore, has not been my first concern. That I have given him cause to think about the issues I have raised, whether he is for or against any of my particular interpretations, has been.

No one who has known sincere contrition over how he has thought, felt or acted would ever say it was a pleasant or easygoing experience. Contrition is not a joy; there is no bliss in it, no rapture, no ecstasy, no laughter. It is an experience, rather, that requires a healthy sense of realism: an ability to look at oneself with a certain hard and unsparing vision. Its content, after all, is the wrong, the sin one has committed: a content before which our vision often tends to become myopic, obscured and out of focus. Clarity is rarely shadowed when contemplating the virtue we possess; but it is easily blurred when thinking of our vice. This is a truth, I imagine, with which we are all more than enough acquainted.

It is in recognition of this truth, therefore, that I have traced throughout these reflections the one theme above all others of personal responsibility. In each of the chapters this single note has rung true: I must recognize that the sin

I regret and the amendment I promise are each facets of a responsibility that is clearly my own. As soon as I try to diffuse this responsibility—either by not taking it seriously enough, or by trying to shoulder it off on others—I have to that extent departed from what it means to be contrite.

But while I cannot share my responsibility for sin with others, this does not mean that I am not in need of them. Starting with our discussion of the "I" who confesses contrition in chapter one, to our discussion of the "I" who asks prayers in chapter three, this note too has rung true: I cannot stand alone in my contrition, proudly certain of my self-sufficiency in overcoming vice and expressing virtue. If I alone am responsible for my sin, I can be contrite for it only in league with others. I am dependent upon them for their aid and example, their humility and generosity in rectifying what is wrong in my life. In contrition no man is an island, entire of himself; he must responsibly seek the help of others, his "brothers and sisters," in amending the sin he regrets.

Now if contrition is set within a Christian framework, as it has been in this book, then it is obvious to whom the contrite individual must first turn in seeking help: namely, the person, the words and deeds, of Jesus. It is the example of the Lord that catalyzes the regret one experiences for wrongdoing, and then provides the guide for amending it. This example, of course, is found preeminently in the witness of the New Testament, but also, and more concretely, in the Christlikeness manifested by our brothers and sisters, the saints, both dead and still living. What contrition demands is an *effective, faithful* responsibility toward those who have gone before us, and those still living by our sides, whose lives demonstrate those virtues we wish to make our own.

Contrition is a lifelong activity. A point is never

reached where the individual can say: I have amended all my sin; I have finished my striving; I am Christlike. Being like Christ is a goal that is ever before us; we can approximate but never fully attain it. There will always be something in the way we think, feel or act that will demand our regret and need our amendment. Thus we have more than once described contrition as a *task*. Contrition is a labor, an effort motivated by that striving for Christlikeness which only death will end. St. Paul captures the idea best in Colossians 1:28: "The mystery is Christ among you, your hope of glory: this is the Christ we proclaim, this is the wisdom in which we thoroughly train everyone, and instruct everyone, to make them all perfect in Christ."

This saying of St. Paul brings us to a final dimension of the responsibility that contrition demands. If I must responsibly seek the assistance of other living persons in becoming Christlike, then they may seek the same assistance from me. I must strive not only to learn Christlikeness from these others, I must strive as well to manifest it to them. Between myself and others contrition establishes a relationship of mutual responsibility. As I look to them to see the image of Christ concretely expressed, so they look to me for the same reason; as I expect to find this image in them, so they expect to find it in me. As they to some degree fail me when they do not fulfill this expectation, so I fail them when I do not fulfill it. Contrition requires reciprocity, a shared spirit of docility: As I must learn Christ from you, so you must learn Christ from me.

This reciprocity in contrition—this mutual willingness to learn from and to teach one another what it means to regret the sin we have committed and to amend our lives according to the example of Christ—defines a basic characteristic of that living community we call the Christian church. Yet it is a characteristic that is often overlooked in discussions of the church, so that I have tried in this book to bring it to fuller awareness. We are not only a community capable of being saved—saved by God's grace, saved by Christ and the witness of his followers. We are also a community capable of sin—able to refuse God's grace, or ignore Christ and the witness of his followers. Together we must live with both these capacities, admitting, as we said in chapter two, that we are born in fault. Together we must strive to strengthen the first capacity and lessen the second.

If we each strive to make the above awareness our own, then the "sting" of having to confess contrition will be largely pulled. If we all become aware that each of us possesses virtue we must nourish and sustain, and vice we must regret and amend, then contrition becomes a communal responsibility; that is, the responsibility of all. My sin would then isolate me from others no more than my virtue does. All suffer the same failure when they fail to be Christlike; all must be contrite for it. I am here not an exception, therefore; I am a participant. It would take a blind and rampant despair to cause the thought that I am alone in my vice, just as it would take a blind and rampant pride to cause the thought that I am alone in my virtue.

It is our togetherness as a community, then, a church, that gives contrition its consolation. In the awareness that we are all centered on Christ, and striving for Christlikeness, we find the motive that makes contrition for sin a positive and creative act, a task and need willingly undertaken. In being forgiven and forgiving the sins that plague us all, in being helped and helping one another toward Christlikeness, we have the bond, the spirit that makes us one.

But this bond, this spirit that unites us, will soon dissolve if at its heart there is not found selflessness, and its two favored children, generosity and humility. It is of the first of these children that St. Paul therefore writes: "The point is this: he who sows sparingly will also reap sparingly, and he who sows bountifully will also reap bountifully. Each must do as he has made up his mind, not reluctantly or grudgingly. For God loves a cheerful giver" (2 Cor 9:6-7). And it is of the second of these children that St. Peter therefore writes: "Wrap yourselves in humility to be servants of each other, for God refuses the proud but will always favor the humble" (1 Pt 5:5).